**Marco Meirovitz** is the well-known educator and game inventor (more than 35 million of his MASTERMIND® have been sold around the world). His system to improve thinking skills by playing games has been used successfully in many countries by both children and adults.

**Dr. Paul I. Jacobs**, a psychologist involved in education, has conducted research for many years on the improvement of thinking skills. Among his previous books is *Up the IQ!: How to Raise Your Child's Intelligence.*

# Brain Muscle Builders

## Games to Increase Your Natural Intelligence

Marco Meirovitz

Paul I. Jacobs

A SPECTRUM BOOK

Prentice-Hall, Inc., Englewood Cliffs, New Jersey 07632

*Library of Congress Cataloging in Publication Data*

Meirovitz, Marco.
  Brain muscle builders.

  "A Spectrum Book."
  1. Educational games.  2. Creative thinking (Education)  I. Jacobs, Paul I.  II. Title.
GV1480.M44   1983      371.3′97      83–13913
ISBN 0–13–080978–0 (pbk.)

This book is available at a special discount
when ordered in bulk quantities. Contact
Prentice-Hall, Inc., General Publishing Division,
Special Sales, Englewood Cliffs, N.J. 07632.

A SPECTRUM BOOK

Printed in the United States of America

10  9  8  7  6  5  4  3  2  1

## ISBN 0-13-080978-0 {PBK.}

Prentice-Hall International, Inc., *London*
Prentice-Hall of Australia Pty. Limited, *Sydney*
Prentice-Hall Canada Inc., *Toronto*
Prentice-Hall of India Private Limited, *New Delhi*
Prentice-Hall of Japan, Inc., *Tokyo*
Prentice-Hall of Southeast Asia Pte. Ltd., *Singapore*
Whitehall Books Limited, Wellington, *New Zealand*
Editora Prentice-Hall Do Brasil Ltda., *Rio de Janeiro*

# Contents

# Preface

If you want to play games, enjoy yourself, and improve your thinking skills all at the same time, this book is for you!

This book contains games presented in a way that makes you want to play, helps you learn how to play, and gives you practice applying what you learn from the games to other life situations.

The book helps you directly increase your abilities in Deduction, Induction, Strategy, and Creative Thinking. You will also learn many other skills (decision-making, seeing ahead, setting priorities, taking risks, prediction, patience, and speed of reaction) that play a part in the games of this book even though we don't devote separate chapters to them. And you will see how these skills can be applied in your daily life.

You will find that improving your thinking skills by using this book gives you other benefits as well: a gain in self-confidence, a loss of "fear of thinking," the further development of your personality, and better self-understanding.

We present a carefully prepared program for improving thinking skills in a step-by-step way. Everyone can find his or her own level to begin. It can be used by people of all ages, and people without any special background or knowledge. It can be used by teachers, by parents, by groups of friends, and by individuals. The entire family can play, have fun and learn together!

You may be one of many parents whose child has trouble in a particular school subject, such as mathematics, or who is generally not interested in schoolwork. If so, you can first capture your child's interest with these games, and then actually see your child improve in important skill areas with your help.

As a teacher, of course, you are even more likely to have some students who can benefit from playing these games.

We believe that playing games is an ideal way to improve thinking skills. First of all, games are fun. Both children and adults will eagerly play games for hours.

Here are some of the many other advantages of playing games:

- Games contain all the basic elements of our everyday activities in work, school and home: planning ahead, decision-making, setting priorities, dealing with people whose goals are incompatible with yours, and so forth.

- Because games are fun, you enjoy yourself while you improve your thinking skills.

- Games can be set up for play at different levels according to the players' abilities. In this way everyone can participate and enjoy playing. You can begin a game at a level you are comfortable with, and gradually increase your skill and your self-confidence.

- When you play games you are actively exercising your thinking skills. Just as you can't learn tennis as well by talking or reading about it as you can by playing it, you can't develop your thinking skills without being forced to think.

- Playing games is a social process in which players learn to communicate, cooperate and compete.

- Research has shown the value of games for teaching. Most schools and universities use simulation games as an effective instructional method.

- Playing games can be a profitable and fun-filled way to spend our increasing leisure time.

- Games provide a better opportunity for the educator or psychologist to observe a student's intelligence in action than does the more artificial and anxiety-laden setting of an intelligence test.

- Games give you an opportunity to use your imagination, to fantasize, and to try out new roles.

- Through games we can teach, learn, enlarge our experience in life, and develop our personalities.

Among the games in this book are those that have entertained people in many different cultures for hundreds, and in some cases, thousands of years. We have put in some modern favorites, and created some new games just for the book.

Yet all these games can be played with just the board and cards that are included in the back of the book, and in some cases, with pencil, paper, and a few pennies, nickels, and dimes from your pocket.

There are a number of advantages of using *ordinary playing cards*.

- Card games are familiar to both children and adults.

- The same games are played and enjoyed around the world.

- Ordinary playing cards are among the least expensive of educational materials.

- You can play the same games no matter what language you speak.

This book, then, will show you how to increase your deduction, induction, strategy, and creative thinking skills by playing games, and how to develop your habit of applying these skills in everyday life. Your thinking skills, just like your athletic skills, can be improved by proper exercise. We invite you to see how playing games is an enjoyable and effective way to exercise the "muscles of your mind."

We welcome your comments and suggestions regarding this book so that we can make the next edition even more useful. Please write to M. Meirovitz/Paul I. Jacobs
51 Patton Avenue
Apt. 3
Princeton, NJ 08540
USA

# Introduction

Exercising your "Muscles of the Mind"
—Thinking skills and intelligence
—Types of thinking skills

The fun way to exercise the muscles of the mind
—The Game of Life

This book as a gymnasium of the mind

## EXERCISING YOUR "MUSCLES OF THE MIND"

If you want to play games, to enjoy yourself, and to improve your thinking skills—all at the same time—then this book is for you! That's a tall claim. So let's see how the book can do what we say it can do. . . .

We take for granted that you can play better tennis if you practice and that you'll improve even more if you have the right coaching. Some of us may be "born athletes," but *all* of us can benefit from practice. We also take for granted that being in good physical shape is important. With regular exercise, we stay healthy. If the exercise takes the form of doing something we enjoy, such as playing tennis, dancing, skating, and the like, so much the better. By practicing, we can go from awkwardness to competence in a physical activity. We tend to engage in the activity more often and, as a result, feel better about ourselves. In any kind of activity, each of us doesn't need to become a champion or superstar. We just need to feel comfortable doing it, and we need to get enjoyment from doing it.

What we have just said applies to having good thinking skills too: You can think better if you practice under the right coaching. Since we think all the time, let's do it well and become more productive in all aspects of our lives. Let's become comfortable with the process, enjoy it, and get better at it. All this means that we must exercise the "muscles of the mind."

Do *you* exercise your muscles of the mind regularly? Many people do not. They are afraid of thinking. They say to themselves, "This is too hard. I can't do it. And I don't want others to see I can't do it." It's *safer* not to try something. Then neither you nor anybody else knows you can't do it. As a result, we often behave as if our thinking ability is asleep. Yet if we let ourselves, we all *can* use our minds much better than we usually do. If we only can get rid of our fear, we can wake our minds up. For example, many people say, "I can't do math. I have no head for figures." What they're really saying is, "I've had poor instruction. I've been embarrassed by what I couldn't do. And I'm not going to put myself in a situation where I get embarrassed like that again." Recently educators are beginning to appreciate the reality of "math anxiety," which can be successfully treated. In a more general sense, the "fear of thinking" can be treated too, and, as you shall see, the treatment is a pleasant one.

Another group of people also fail to exercise their muscles of their minds regularly. They are not *afraid* of thinking; it just seems like hard work. Are you one of them? If so, you will see that exercising your muscles of the mind can be fun!

## THINKING SKILLS AND INTELLIGENCE

Just what are these "thinking skills" we're talking about? Many people connect "thinking skills" with "intelligence." In fact, both dictionaries and psychologists have trouble defining intelligence exactly. Here's what various dictionaries say about the meaning of the word:

- "The ability to learn or understand from experience; ability to acquire and retain knowledge; mental ability . . ."
- "The ability to respond quickly and successfully to a new situation: use of the faculty of reason in solving problems; directing conduct, etc., effectively."
- "The capacity to acquire and apply knowledge, the faculty of thought and reason."

The dictionaries speak of intelligence as a capacity, an ability, and a faculty. They further define these terms as follows:

- *Capacity*—"the power of receiving and holding knowledge, impressions, etc., mental ability."
- *Faculty*—"power or ability to do some particular thing."
- *Ability*—"power to do something physical or mental."

Other dictionaries define capacity and faculty as ability, ability as talent, and talent as ability. And what do they say intelligence is the ability, capacity, or faculty to do? It is to learn or understand, to acquire and retain knowledge, to apply knowledge, to think, to reason, and so on.

Some psychologists frankly acknowledge their confusion about what they mean by "intelligence." In 1927 psychologist Charles Spearman said that "intelligence" had become "a mere vocal sound, a word with so many meanings that it finally had none." And another expert, T. R. Miles, has commented: "Any sentence starting 'intelligence is . . .' justifiably arouses one's suspicions." Yet the dictionaries' and the psychologists' definitions *do* have a common theme: Intelligence includes *the ability to adapt to new situations and to solve problems in a changing environment.*

Such an ability, despite the reluctance of many people to develop it, is more necessary today than ever before. There's no doubt that today's world is much more complex than it was twenty or even ten years ago. To get along in this constantly changing world, we *must* improve our thinking skills.

Our aim in writing this book, therefore, is to show you how to exercise and improve your thinking skills, and to transfer the principles you learn to your own daily activities. If we succeed only in making you *more aware of your own thinking*, we will have taken a big step toward making you a more effective thinker and a person better able to meet the challenge of change.

## TYPES OF THINKING SKILLS

In recent years psychologists have begun to agree that intelligence includes many different thinking skills and that what you can do with your mind depends on the experiences you've had. Our approach fits well with this new point of view: We provide the experiences that will best increase your abilities. We help you to exercise the muscles of your mind. For this first book we have pinpointed four different important thinking skills. We show you:

- *Deductive Logic*: How to put together separate but related facts, to eliminate irrelevant information, and to reach a conclusion that must be so.
- *Inductive Logic*: How to discover rules by carefully observing what is similar and different among many events.
- *Strategy*: How to make plans and organize things to reach your goal.
- *Creative Thinking*: How to come up with new and different ideas.

In this book you can concentrate on each skill separately, just as you might, for example, separately practice serving, forehand strokes, and backhand strokes to improve your tennis game. Of course, these skills do not exist in isolation: You are creative when you think inductively, you use logic when you plan strategy, and so on. In addition, many other skills play a part in the games in this book: decision making, seeing ahead, setting priorities, taking risks, prediction, patience, and speed of reaction. You will be learning these as well, but we don't devote separate chapters to them.

## THE FUN WAY TO EXERCISE THE MUSCLES OF THE MIND

Playing games is an ideal way to improve thinking skills. First of all, games are fun. Children play games spontaneously for hours. Adults do the same, if they can find the time. It's more fun to learn logic by figuring out which cards are in your opponent's hand than to learn a logical syllogism such as:

All dogs are animals.
Fido is a dog.
Therefore Fido is an animal.

Let's then take advantage of our strong drive to play and make playing games a time of learning. Here are the advantages of developing your thinking skills by playing games:

- Games contain all the basic elements of our everyday activities in work, school, and home: planning ahead, decision making, setting priorities, dealing with people whose goals are incompatible with yours, and so on.
- The rules of a game give you a structure within which to work toward your goals, to resolve personal problems and conflicts, and to develop your personality.
- You actively learn thinking skills. You can't learn tennis as well by talking or reading about it as you can by playing it. Accordingly, you can't develop your thinking skills without being forced to think.
- You also learn to behave well in a social setting, to cooperate with others, to obey rules, and to propose new rules. You can't always win in life, and games teach you how to lose gracefully.
- Because games are fun, they attract a great number of participants. Teaching becomes easier because the learners are better motivated.
- Games can be set up for play at different levels according to the player's abilities. Everyone can participate and enjoy playing. By beginning a game at a comfortable level and gradually increasing your skill, you increase your self-confidence.
- Research has shown the value of games for teaching. Most schools and universities use simulation games as an effective instructional method.
- Games develop the personality and character of the players. Our leisure time is increasing, and playing games can be a profitable and *fun-filled* way to spend it.
- Games give you an opportunity to use your imagination, to fantasize, to try out new roles, and to escape from unpleasant realities.
- Through games we can teach, learn, and enlarge our experience in life.

## THE GAME OF LIFE

Games have all these advantages for us because *games reflect life*. The games we play reflect the culture we live in or, in some cases, the culture our ancestors lived in. For example, a picture from an Egyptian tomb painting of around 1800 B.C. shows what might be two games essentially the same as our Chinese checkers and checkers today. How did such games originate? We don't know for sure when, where, and why games were first invented. The earliest games were probably sports that hunters played to strengthen their bodies for the hunt. Perhaps, as time went by, the leader of a primitive group learned to prepare for a battle by outlining the battlefield on the ground, placing small stones on the ground to represent opposing forces, and then moving stones around to show the troops the battle plan. Such a method might have helped to communicate the plan to those who didn't have a common language. And by playing with different arrangements of the stones, the leader might eventually try out and discard some poor strategies without actually using them on the battlefield. From this very practical beginning, people may have discovered the fun of moving small objects according to definite rules within certain boundaries. And they may have begun to enjoy games for their own sake. A game that has survived and evolved in many cultures over hundreds of years—and in some cases thousands—demonstrates its basic entertainment appeal.

Such a game may also help people to learn survival skills in both competitive and cooperative situations. The competitive situations we face in daily life, of course, have changed over the centuries from simple physical survival to much more complex social, economic, and interpersonal problems. As a result, more

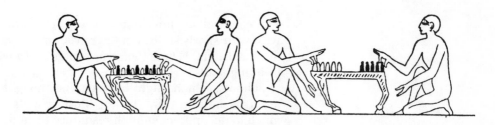

abstract, intellectual games have developed and evolved to help us deal with our modern civilization. Further, most life situations impose limits on what we can and cannot do, rules that tell us what "moves" we can and cannot make, what boundaries we cannot exceed. This is what we mean when we say games reflect life.

Let's look at some of these contemporary situations.

In one type of competitive situation, you are trying to reach a goal, despite obstacles or restraints in the environment. Your success depends on your finding a way around the obstacles. Other people's actions may affect you, but they are basically pursuing their own goals and not trying to get in your way. For example, you are driving to the beach and want to avoid heavy traffic, or you are applying to be admitted to a highly selective college.

In another set of situations, you are competing with other people to reach the *same* goal. In such a case, you try to plan things so that you win and they lose. For example, you are competing with co-workers in the same office for a promotion that has just opened up, or you are attempting to get the one "A" grade that the instructor will give in the course.

In still another set of situations, the competition is on the level of *destroy or be destroyed*. If you fail to win, you don't survive. As an example, you are running a political campaign, where you must receive at least 10 percent of the vote or your party will be abolished. In another instance, you are the head of a military mission behind enemy lines.

Each of these kinds of situations has analogs—that is, games with similar structures—that you will meet in the Strategy chapter.

## THIS BOOK AS A GYMNASIUM OF THE MIND

You can find a gymnasium in every school to get help with your sports skills, but "gymnasiums of the mind" don't exist yet. Where then can you get help with your thinking skills?

Schools, which might be your first thought, cannot teach us how to think better. Most schools have too much to do, and not enough resources to do it. Schools must teach so many facts for the students to learn and remember, that they can barely keep up with just the teaching of facts. To make the school's task tougher, more facts are being accumulated every day. It seems as if, unless human progress comes to a stop, the schools will never be able to pass on to us all the facts we need.

Some educators see this situation clearly. They recognize that teaching people *how to discover facts* and *how to use them* is more important than just teaching the facts themselves. Yet these educators face two problems:

1. The schools are generally not prepared to teach thinking skills. Curriculum materials are lacking. Many teachers are not sufficiently trained to teach thinking skills, and they are afraid to try.

2. The educational system is set up to teach subjects, not skills. The only skills taught apart from subjects are the skills taught in physical education classes. The schools are under pressure to continue teaching subjects, and not to be diverted to the teaching of thinking skills.

In this book we address both problems:

1. We present a carefully prepared program for teaching thinking skills in a step-by-step way that can be used by teachers, by parents, by groups of friends, and by individuals. It can be used by people of all ages and by people without any special background knowledge. In this way, we directly overcome the first problem.

2. As people both inside and outside the schools experience success with the book, another pressure builds up from parents, educators, and the community: to make room for the teaching of thinking skills in the schools. This pressure will help to overcome the second problem.

In this special kind of gymnasium, the games must make you *want* to play, help you learn *how* to play, and give you practice *applying* what you learn in the game situation to other life situations. We have therefore chosen games with educational value that have entertained people in many different cultures for hundreds, and in some cases thousands, of years. In all these games, *your thinking*, not *chance*, makes the difference. We have added some modern favorites, and created some new games that are fun to play just for this book. All together, these games can give you unlimited hours of fun. We have also adapted these games to a playing card format. Here are the advantages of using ordinary *playing cards* for these games:

- Card games are familiar to both children and adults.
- The same games are played and enjoyed around the world.
- You can play the same card games no matter which language you speak.
- With inexpensive cards you can play an unlimited number of different games.
- For all these reasons, card games play a prominent role in the plans for the Olympic Games of the Mind being developed by M. Meirovitz.

The format of these games also tries to present things as simply as possible. Some games, like chess, don't appeal to many people because they seem too complicated to learn. Such games may seem "too complicated" because they have many confusing "arbitrary" rules. Beginners must therefore struggle to understand and remember the rules, and they cannot appreciate the goals, strategy, and beauty of the game. Even a "complicated" game, however, is based on certain simple, easy-to-learn elements.

Using the physical exercise analogy, look at our approach this way. If you try to break a whole bundle of sticks all at once, you won't succeed—and you won't be strengthening your muscles much either. Yet if you take hold of just one or two sticks, you'll have no trouble breaking them. You will strengthen your muscles, and you'll have a method for attacking the whole bundle of sticks. In the future, you will also have stronger muscles and a method for attacking other bundles of sticks.

The same thing applies to thinking skills, games, and the muscles of the mind. In this book we first show you a simple version of a "complicated" game, so that you catch on to the rules easily and immediately enjoy playing. Then, so that you can move on when you have mastered the simple version, we gradually introduce "complications," such as more playing pieces, a larger playing field, and additional rules. You decide when you are ready for a greater challenge. In this way you learn the basic features of a great many enjoyable games that have much educational value.

This book would have purpose enough if it just introduced you to many new games that you enjoyed playing. But, as you know by now, we want to go beyond that. We want you to learn some general principles from these games that will *improve your thinking skills, and also show you how to transfer these principles to real-life situations*. In this way we involve more and more people in exercising the muscles of their minds by playing games. The intellectual potential of the individual and of the nation is thus raised.

From our experience, though, people need help carrying over what they learn in one situation to other situations. Each major chapter of this book therefore provides an *applications* section. In this section, you can apply the skills you've learned to other situations that we present, and you are also given suggestions on applying these skills in your own life.

# How to Use the Book

*About the book*
　—The four major chapters of games:
　　　Deductive Logic Games
　　　Inductive Logic Games
　　　Strategy Games of Movement
　　　Strategy Games of Conflict
　—Groups and levels of games

*The way to play*
　—Finding your own level
　—Games vs. puzzles
　—Having fun with games

*What you need*

*Rules common to all games*

## ABOUT THE BOOK

The games in this book are organized into four major chapters:

- D = *Deductive Logic*
- I = *Inductive Logic*
- SM = *Strategy Games of Movement*
- SC = *Strategy Games of Conflict*

Each chapter contains:

- an introduction to the skill,
- groups of games and their rules of playing,
- sample games described,
- applications of principles from the games, and
- problems for you to solve, with solutions at the end of the book.

Each chapter helps you build up one important "muscle" of the mind, and it can be read and used by itself. We begin each chapter by describing the major skill it deals with: what the skill is, how it is used, why it is important.

The games in each chapter are organized into *groups*. Each group of games is self-contained: *you can play the games in one group without having played the games in the other groups.* All the games in the same group have similar rules, and they are presented in three levels:

- LL = *Low Level*
- ML = *Medium Level*
- HL = *High Level*

These levels refer to how the games *within a* group compare in difficulty. They do *not* refer to a player's general ability level. You may be quite comfortable with a *high-level* game in one group, and not yet be ready for a *high-level* game in another group.

Each game is described in a ruled-off section under the heading "Rules of the Game." Above this heading, the game code tells you where in the group the game belongs. In this code, the letter tells you the major skill. For example, "D" means Deductive Logic. The first number tells you the group, and the second number the game within the group. Game D 1–4 for instance, means the fourth game in the first group in the Deductive Logic (D) chapter; Game SM 4–1 means the first game in the fourth group in the Strategy Games of Movement (SM) chapter. The level of the game is given in parentheses: I 2–3 (HL) means that the third game in the second group in the Inductive Logic chapter is at the higher level. (HL).

After the four major chapters on games, we show you in Chapter 5 how you can apply creative thinking in games and in real-life situations. Chapter 6 shows you how you can apply *all* the skills you have learned from the games to real-life situations. The Appendix contains a warm-up exercise game for your mind and a section on applying probability to games.

**THE WAY TO PLAY**

Always start with the first game in a group. This game is analyzed for you, the rules are the most thoroughly discussed of all the games in the group, and sample games are provided. If you find that the first game in a group is not challenging enough for you, you can then skip ahead to a later game in the same group. When you find the right level for you within a group of games, stay with it until you have mastered it. Then move on.

As you can see, the book is more like a reference or handbook than one you would read straight through from beginning to end and use only once. You can go through it many times, enjoying and learning from it each time. The book can provide many merry years of fun for everyone in the family—children and grown-ups alike. You may therefore want to dip into the book on many different occasions: on a train or plane ride, when sick, when friends drop in, when you're looking for an activity to break the ice at a gathering where people don't know each other well, to make new friends, entertain old friends, and so on.

You can play some of the games, particularly in the first group of the Strategy chapter, by yourself. Some are more like puzzles than like games. (The book is, however, fundamentally a *game* book, not a *puzzle* book. A puzzle has one route to the solution. In a game, however, a different set of events may occur each time it's played, even with the same rules. You can enjoy the same game many times.) Other games can be played with two, three, four, or even more players. Some are intended for two to four players, but we also point out, or you can see yourself, how just one person can play.

After you play a game, discuss it with the other players. As you enter the minds of other people and see how they think, you can improve your own thinking and playing. We shall deal with this aspect of game playing in more detail in Chapter 6.

After you master a game, change the rules. Create your own games. Among the things you might change are:

- the starting positions of the cards,
- the size of the grid,
- the number of players,
- the number of cards,
- the way the cards are moved,
- the choices each player has,

- how the game is scored,
- what "winning" means,
- time limits, and
- the chance element.

You might even try a rule from one game in a completely different game.

See which changes work (in the sense that they make the game more fun to play) and which changes don't work. In Chapter 6, we show you some of the changes we have thought of, and we discuss further why you should make changes. You can skip ahead to this chapter at any time, returning to it more than once.

Read and work through the Applications section of a chapter after you play the games in it.

## WHAT YOU NEED

To play the games in this book, you need:

1. two decks of cards,
2. a playing board,
3. 32 chess cards, and
4. 24 tokens.

Blue deck
Red deck

### The Cards

The backs of the two cards should be distinguishable—different colors, different shades, and so on. In this book, we refer to the two common colors, red and blue. Each should be a complete standard deck, with aces to kings in clubs, diamonds, hearts, and spades, and two jokers. For our purposes, the jacks, queens, and kings are called "picture cards."

In some games the ranks (or numbers) and suits of the cards are not important. If two different kinds of cards are needed, use the cards face down, making the red-backs and blue-backs the two kinds of cards. If *three* or *four* kinds of cards are needed, then turn the cards face up, and each *suit* can be a different kind of card.

### The Board

One board is used for all the games, whose two sides are shown on page 17. For most games, you use the side shown at the top. For checkers and chess in the Strategy Games of Conflict chapter, you use the side shown at the bottom.

On both sides, the board is divided into 8 rows of 8 squares each. We call a board that is divided up this way a *grid*. Each row, from left to right, is labeled 1, 2, 3 . . . 8. Each top-to-bottom column is labeled A, B, C . . . H. These numbers and letters are the *coordinates*, which we use to refer to a particular square. For example, in the diagram below, the three of hearts is in square B5, and the queen of spades is in G6.

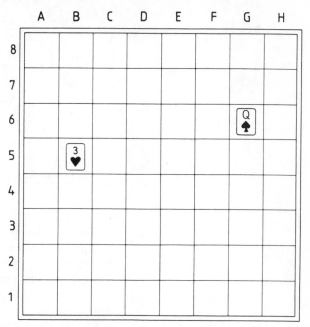

The side of the board used for checkers and chess has an extra feature: Each square is either white or grey, and the two colors alternate.

The "Materials Needed" part of "Rules of the Game" section always tells you the size grid you need for a particular game. In some games, you use the entire 8×8 grid. In other games, you use only part of it, such as a 3×3 grid. When you need a grid smaller than 8×8, mark off the boundaries of the grid with the grey cards (the backs of the chess cards, see below). For example, in the following diagram (page 18), the description of the game calls for a 3×4 grid. The borders of this grid are marked off with the grey cards. Marking off a grid smaller than 8×8, always start at the lower left-hand corner (square A1). Then the coordinates of the area you use will always match the coordinates in our description and in the analysis of the game.

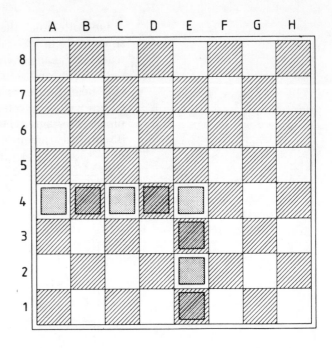

### The Chess Cards
The chess cards are used only for the chess games described in the Strategy Games of Conflict chapter. The back of each card is colored grey.

### The Tokens
You need 24 tokens in each of three colors (72 in all). In place of tokens, you may use coins, buttons, or similar items.

## RULES COMMON TO ALL GAMES

Some games require a player in a special role, such as dealer, code-maker, code-breaker, rule-maker or rule-finder. In each such game, the deck is shuffled, and each player takes out one card. The player with the card with the highest *rank* takes on the special role. For this purpose, the ace is highest, followed by king, queen, jack, 10, down to 2 (the lowest). In case of ties, spades are highest among the suits, followed by hearts, diamonds, and clubs (lowest). When the game ends, another player takes on the special role. The game

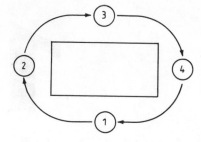

should be played until each player is in the special role an equal number of times.

In games where players rotate turns, the player to the dealer's left goes first. If there is no dealer, each player takes a card from the shuffled deck, and player with the higher card goes first. If players are seated around a table, then the order of playing rotates clockwise. If not, then the player with the next highest card goes second, and so on. In the game descriptions, player *A* is the first player, *B* the second player, and so on.

In games where cards are moved on the grid, a player who touches a card must move it if it is legal to do so.

All cards should be placed the long way up and down on the grid—not some long way up and down, and others long way left to right.

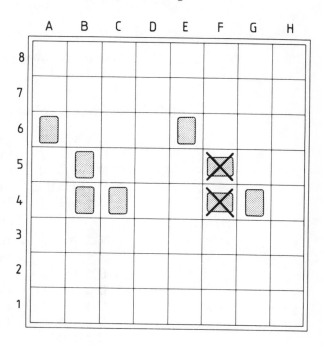

# 1

# Deductive Logic

I once had a green rash on my arm and went to the doctor, who frowned when he examined me. For a long time he seemed puzzled. Then he asked, "Have you ever had this before?"

"Yes," I replied.

"Oh well," he said triumphantly, "then you've got it again."

This story illustrates a poor use of deductive logic: *If* I had a green rash before and if I have it now, *then* I've got it again. The doctor used all the information he could get from the situation and through deductive logic reached his "diagnosis." I used all the information I could get from the situation and found another doctor.

When properly used, deductive logic is an important muscle of the mind. Often we are in an everyday life situation with many possibilities to explore. We need an organized, systematic way to put together separate facts that are related to one another and reach a conclusion that must be so. Here are some examples:

- My car won't start. Many different things may be causing the problem. But if the engine turns over, I can eliminate the battery as the source of the problem.

- Six guests will be coming to dinner, and I want to serve the same meal to each one. I know how to prepare many different dishes. As I find out my guests' food preferences (for example, is anyone a vegetarian?), and what foods are available (are strawberries in season?), I begin to narrow down my choices.

- To discover who is guilty in the "whodunit" mystery story and in real-life police work, a pool of suspects is established, and information is collected to eliminate all but one of the suspects.

- If I know that one of three cards face down in a row is a queen, and that it isn't the one on the left or the one on the right, then I know it must be the one in the middle.

In each of these situations, you begin with a question:

- Why do I have this rash?
- Why won't my car start?
- What shall I serve my dinner guests?
- Who is the murderer?
- Which face-down card is the queen?

You have many possible answers, and you obtain new information to eliminate possibilities and find the one correct answer.

You can apply deductive logic to each of these situations. The same kind of thinking that helps you to discover which card is the queen can help you to determine why you have the rash, why you car won't start, what to serve your dinner guests, and who the murderer is.

In this chapter we show you how to build up your deductive logic ability by playing card games. A common theme of *all* these games is how to eliminate possibilities in an organized, systematic way to reach an answer that must be so. After you have developed your deductive logic ability, we also show you how to apply this ability in other situations.

## D 1–1 (LL)
### RULES OF THE GAME

*Aim of the Game*: With visual help, to find out the rank and suit of one secret card from a group of 32 cards.

*Number of Players*: Two

*Materials Needed*: The aces through 8s from both decks.

*Preparation*: Each deck is shuffled separately. *A* looks at top card of red deck, which becomes the secret card (or the *code*) that *B* must find out. Then blue deck is dealt out face up in four rows of eight cards each.

*How to Play*: *B* asks a question about the secret card which can be answered by "yes" or "no" only. After getting an answer from *A*, *B* takes away those cards that can be eliminated. The game continues in the same way with further questions and answers until *B* finds out the secret card. Then the players switch roles.

*Scoring*: *A* receives one token for each question asked. After each player has had an equal number of times in each role, the player with more tokens wins.

## D 1–2 (LL)
Same as D 1–1, but start with a *full* deck of fifty-two cards, instead of 32 cards.

## D 1–3 (ML)
Same as D 1–1, but blue deck is *not* deal out. *B* will not see the eliminated cards taken away and must keep the information in his/her head.

## D 1–4 (ML)
Same as D 1–1, but start with a *full* deck that is not dealt out. *B* must keep information in his/her head.

## D 1–5 (HL)
Players agree on a category, such as *objects in the room*, *famous people in history*, or *geographical places*, instead of playing cards. *A* writes down one secret object (or person or place) that fits the category, and *B* asks questions about it that can be answered only by "yes" or "no." Otherwise rules are the same as D 1–3.

Let's see how a game of D 1–1 might go. Suppose the secret card from the red deck is the three of hearts, and the blue deck is laid out as shown.

Starting position

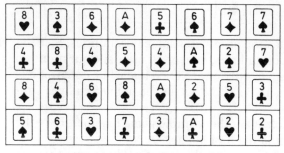

Is it a club? No.

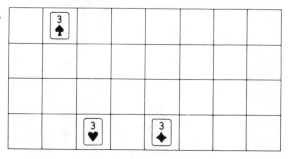

Is it higher than a 4? No.

Is it a 3 or 4? Yes.

Is it a 4? No.

Is it a red card? Yes.

Is it a heart? Yes.

It's the 3 of hearts.

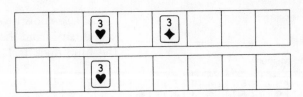

Each question eliminates some possibilities. Starting with 32 possibilities, player *B* uses six questions to reduce them to only one. Notice that a "no" answer lets you eliminate possibilities just as much as a "yes" answer does.

Let's look at another sample game together. Here the secret card is the 5 of spades.

Is it possible to find the secret card in *fewer* than six questions?

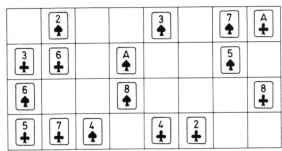

Is it a red card? No.

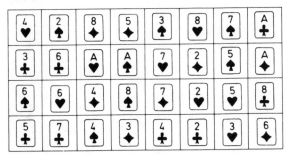

Is it an even number? No.

Is it a 5 or higher? Yes.

Is it a club? No.

Is it the 7 of spades? No.

Then it's the 5 of spades.

In this case five questions were enough.

Play this game until you are able to always locate the secret card quickly. Notice that your progress is steadiest when you ask a question that eliminates *half* the cards, no matter whether the answer is "yes" or "no."

## CHOOSING CARDS

In the next group of games, you must find out *more than one* secret card by eliminating possibilities.

## D 2–1 (LL)
### RULES OF THE GAME

*Aim of the Game*: To find the ranks of some secret cards out of many (2 out of 5), by choosing which cards you want to get information about.

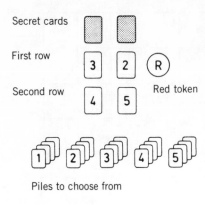

Secret cards

First row

Second row

Red token

Piles to choose from

*Number of Players*: Two

*Materials Needed*: The aces through 5s (1–5) from both decks; red tokens.

*How to Play*: All the cards of the same rank are put into a separate pile face up on the table. *A* (as *code-maker*) picks up one card from each pile, chooses two of these five to be the secret cards (the cards in the *code*), and places them face down on the table without the other player seeing what they are. *B* (as *code-breaker*) chooses two cards from the face-up piles to get information about, and places them in a row *below* the secret cards. *A* places one red token alongside this row for each card in it that has the same rank as one of the secret cards.

The game continues, with *B* choosing further rows and *A* giving information, until *B* finds out the ranks of the two secret cards. Then they switch roles: *B* becomes the code-maker and *A* the code-breaker.

*Scoring: A* (the code-maker) receives one token for each face-up row needed. Play three, five, or ten rounds. The player with more tokens wins.

*Remark*: The *code-maker* gets more points for giving more information. It's best for the *code-breaker* to find out the secret cards by using as few rows as possible.

### D 2–2 (LL)
Seme as D 2–1, but *A* chooses *three*, instead of two, secret cards.

### D 2–3 (LL)
Same as D 2–1, but *A* chooses *three*, instead of two, secret cards, and use the 1–7, instead of 1–5, from both decks.

### D 2–4 (ML)
Same as D 2–1, but *A* chooses *three*, instead of two, secret cards, and use the 1–10, instead of 1–5, from both decks.

### D 2–5 (ML)
Same as D 2–1, but *A* chooses *three*, instead of two, secret cards, and use all the cards from both decks.

### D 2–6 (HL)
Same as D 2–1, but *A* chooses *four*, instead of two, secret cards, and use all the cards from both decks.

Now we will give a sample game of D 2–1, 2 out of 5, (LL). You are *A*, the code-maker, and your friend is *B*, the code-breaker. You alone look at the top two cards, and place them face down in a row. Remember that the ranks of these cards ("three" or "five") are important in this game and not their suits ("clubs" or "diamonds"). Any time you forget the ranks of the cards, you can look at them again. But don't show them to your friend.

Suppose your friend selects a 5 and a 3 to get information about on the first "trial" (the first face-up row), and the secret cards are a 1 and a 3. Placing one token alongside the row (for the 3), you would say, "One of these cards [pointing to the face-up cards] is the same as one of these [pointing to the secret cards]. You have to figure out what both of these cards are [pointing again to the secret cards]. Can you do it now?"

5        3 ●

Most people cannot. Only a person with ESP can. The game depends on deductive logic, not on guessing and not on ESP. There is not yet enough information to discover the secret cards through deductive logic.

Your friend might say (guessing), "It's the 5" or "It's the 3." You must say, "You need to know *both* cards. Here's some more information." Your friend now makes a second trial. The cards might now look like this:

5        3 ●<br>2        5

Since neither the 2 nor the 5 is a secret card, you would not place any token alongside this row. Your friend could combine the information from the two trials this way: "From the first row, I know that either the 5 or the 3 (but not both!) is a secret card. From the second row, I know that neither the 2 nor the 5 is a secret card. So the secret card in the first row must be the 3."

Your friend would continue with another row:

5        3 ●<br>2        5<br>1        2 ●

Your friend might now say: "This trial tells me that either the 1 or the 2 (but not both!) is a secret card. I already know from the second trial that the 2 is not a secret card. So the secret card here on the third trial must be the 1. The two secret cards are a 3 and a 1."

Your friend, using deductive logic correctly, reached the right conclusion.

Simple enough? Let's look together at another sample game with the same rules. In this game you are *B*, the *code-breaker*.

Suppose the secret cards are a 5 and a 2, and the cards you select to get information about on the first trial are 3 and 1. No token is put down, and you know neither a 3 nor a 1 is a secret card.

For your second trial you select 2 and 4, and find out that one of them is a secret card. You can't yet tell which.

For the third trial, then, you select a 4, which *might* be a secret card, and a 1, which you know *can't* be a secret card.

|   |   |   |
|---|---|---|
| 3 | 1 |   |
| 2 | 4 | ● |
| 4 | 1 |   |

You find out the 4 is *not* a secret card, and so the secret card on the second trial must be the 2. You know that the 1, 3, and 4 are not secret cards, and the other secret card must therefore be the 5.

### Duplication Allowed Variation

The players may agree before the game to allow the possibility that two (or more) secret cards have the same rank. Then, instead of placing cards face down to indicate the code, the *code-maker* writes down what the secret cards are on a piece of paper, which the *code-breaker* doesn't see.

Let's look at some sample games where duplication is allowed. We will begin to *organize* the information we get from each trial and the deductive thinking we do with that information. In a chart, we will record which cards were selected on each trial, how many tokens were put down, and a summary of what we know so far. Here's how a game might go:

|  | Possibilities 1st Card | 2nd Card |
|---|---|---|
| 1. 1,2 ● | 1,2 | 1,2,3,4,5 |
| 2. 3,4 ● | 1,2 | 3,4 |
| 3. 5,1 | 2 | 3,4 |
| 4. 3,5 ● | 2 | 3 |

On the first trial, you select a 1 and 2, finding out that one of them is a secret card. We show this under "Possibilities" by saying we know the "first" card is either a 1 or a 2. Since duplication is allowed, the "second" card might be a 1, 2, 3, 4, or 5. We arbitrarily call one secret card "first" and the other "second."

For the second trial, you select a 3 and 4, and find out that one of them is a secret card. If one secret card is a 1 or 2, and the other is a 3 or 4, then a 5 can't be a secret card.

On the third trial you want to see whether a 1 or a 2 is a secret card. You combine a 5 (which you already know is *not* a secret card) and a 1 on this trial. You discover the 1 is not a secret card, so the 2 must be. On the fourth trial, working the same way, you find out that the 3 is the other secret card.

Here's how two more games with the same rules might go:

|  | Possibilities 1st Card | 2nd Card |  |
|---|---|---|---|
| 1. 1,2 | 3,4,5 | 3,4,5 |  |
| 2. 3,4 ● ● | 3 | 4 | We were lucky! |

|  | Possibilities 1st Card | 2nd Card |
|---|---|---|
| 1. 1,2 ● | 1,2 | 1,2,3,4,5 |
| 2. 3,4 | 1,2 | 1,2,5 |
| 3. 5,1 | 2 | 2 |

Here are some sample games for D 2–3, three out of seven. Duplication is allowed.

1. 4,6,5 ●
2. 7,3,2 ● ●
3. 4,5,3

At this point you would have enough information to figure out, without guessing, the three secret cards. Do you see how? See if you can figure it out yourself before you read on.

Here's the explanation. The first trial tells us that either a 4, 5, or 6 is a secret card. The second trial tells us that, among 7, 3, and 2, two of them are secret cards, and one is not. The third trial tells us that the 4, 5, and 3 are all *not* secret cards. Therefore, if the target card on the first trial cannot be the 4 or 5, it must be the 6. If on the second trial the 3 is not a secret card, then the 7 and 2 must be. So the three secret cards are 6, 7, and 2.

Here's another example of a game:

1. 6,1,3
2. 4,3,5 ● ●
3. 7,3,1 ●

The first trial tells us that the 6, 1, and 3 are not secret cards. The second trial reveals two secret cards. Since the 3 is not one of them, they must be the 4 and 5. The third trial shows one target card. Since it cannot be the 3 or 1, it must be the 7. So the three secret cards are 4, 5, and 7.

Are you getting the idea? Here's still another example, recorded in a more systematic way. In this case, *no* duplication is allowed.

| | Possibilities | | |
| | 1st Card | 2nd Card | 3rd Card |
| 1. 6,7,5 | 1,2,3,4 | 1,2,3,4 | 1,2,3,4 |
| 2. 2,3,4 ● ● Either | 2 | 3 | 1 |
| or | 2 | 4 | 1 |
| or | 3 | 4 | 1 |
| 3. 1,2,3 ● ● Either | 2 | 4 | 1 |
| or | 3 | 4 | 1 |
| 4. 1, 2, 4 ● ● ● | 2 | 4 | 1 |

Note that, under "Possibilities" for the second trial, the three separate possibilities are that the 4 or the 3 or the 2 is *not* the secret card on that trial.

We have shown you, as a possible aid, one way of keeping track of the information that you get and of the deductive thinking that you do. There are other ways to keep track, both on paper and in your head. You should choose a method that works best for you.

Remember that, although the object of the game is to find out the secret cards by taking as few trials as possible, the purpose of playing the game is to practice deductive logic. Therefore you must not encourage yourself or others to *guess* in place of *thinking*. You might even add a rule that code-breakers must explain how they got the answer, and that the code-makers must be satisfied with the explanations.

## TURNING CARDS AT RANDOM

In this group of games, you again have to find the ranks of the secret cards. But instead of choosing cards to get information about, they are chosen at random for you.

---

### D 3–1 (LL)
**RULES OF THE GAME**

*Aim of the Game:* To find the ranks of some out of many secret cards (three out of seven) by turning cards up at random to get information.

*Number of Players:* Two

*Materials Needed:* The aces through 7s (1–7) from each deck; red tokens.

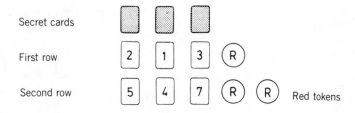

How to Play: A (as code-maker) chooses three cards of different ranks to be the secret cards (the cards in the *code*), placing them face down on the table without B seeing what they are. A then places the top three cards from the shuffled deck face up in a row *below* the secret cards. These are cards that A will give information about. A places one red token alongside this row for each card in it that has the same rank as one of the secret cards. The games continues with A dealing out further rows at random and giving B information about them, until B finds out the code.

*Scoring: A* (the *code-maker*) receives one token for each face-up row needed. Play three, five, or ten rounds. The player with more tokens wins.

### D 3–2 (ML)

Same as D 3–1, but use the 1–10, instead of 1–7.

### D 3–3 (HL)

Same as D 3–1, but *A* chooses *four*, instead of three, secret cards, and use the full decks instead of 1–7.

---

In each game up to now, the *order* of the cards in each row has not made a difference. *One*, *two*, *three* has been the same as *two*, *three*, *one*. But in the next group of games, the *order* of the cards in each row is very important.

---

### D 4–1 (LL)

**RULES OF THE GAME**

*Aim of the Game*: To find out the positions of each card in a row of four cards by choosing cards to get information about.

*Number of Players*: Two

*Materials Needed*: The aces through 4s, (1–4), from both decks; red tokens.

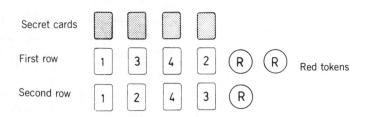

*Preparation*: *A* takes one card of each rank, shuffles them together, and places them face down in a row after looking at the position of each.

*How to Play*: *B* arranges a 1 through 4 in any order in a face-up row below *A*'s row. *A* must give information as to how many of these cards are in the same position as *A*'s own cards. *A* places one token alongside the row for each card in the same position as *A*'s.

The game continues, with *B* choosing further rows and *A* giving information, until *B* finds out the positions of all of *A*'s cards. Then players change roles.

*Scoring: A* (the code-maker) receives one token for each face-up row needed. Play three, five, or ten rounds. The player with more tokens wins.

*Remarks:* The code-maker gets more points for giving more information. It's best for the code-breaker to find out the positions of the secret cards by using as few rows as possible.

More than two players can play at once. Each code-breaker puts down his or her own "Row 1," etc., and receives from *A* four cards face down. Among them is one picture card for each card in that player's row that is in the correct position. In this way each code-breaker gets information only about his or her own rows.

## D 4–2 (ML)
Same as D 4–1, but use 1–6 in a row of 6.

## D 4–3 (HL)
Same as D 4–1, but use 1–10 in a row of 10.

---

Here's how a game might go. Suppose the secret cards are in the order 3,2,4,1.

|  | *Thinking* | *Possibilities* |
|---|---|---|
| 1. 1,2,3,4 ● | Either the 1,2,3, or 4 is in the right position (rp). | Either 1 – – –, or – 2 – –, or – – 3 –, or – – – 4 |
| 2. 2,3,4,1 ● ● | Two of these are in the rp. If the 1 was in the rp in Row 1, then the order must be 1342; no other order fits the Row 2 information. In the same way, if 2, then must be 3241; if 3, must be 2431; if 4, 2314. | Either 1 3 4 2, or 3 2 4 1, or 2 4 3 1, or 2 3 1 4 |

| 3. 2,4,3,1 ● | Only two possible orders for this new information. | Either 3 2 4 1, or 2 3 1 4 |
|---|---|---|

| 4. 3,2,4,1 ● ● ● ● | We've got it! | 3 2 4 1 |

## RANKS AND POSITIONS BY CHOOSING CARDS

In this group of games, you must find out not only the secret cards, but also their positions.

### D 5–1 (LL)
**RULES OF THE GAME**

*Aim of the Game*: To find the code (*ranks* and *positions*) of some out of many (two out of five) secret cards by choosing which cards you want to get information about.

*Number of Players*: Two

*Materials Needed*: The aces through 5s from both decks; green and red tokens.

| The code | | |
|---|---|---|
| First row | 3  2  (R) | Red token |
| Second row | 2  4  (G) | Green token |

*How to Play*: All the cards of the same rank are put into a separate pile face up on the table. *A* (as *code-maker*) picks up one card from each pile, chooses two of these five to be the secret cards (the cards in the *code*), and places them face down on the table without the other player seeing what they are. *B* (as *code-breaker*) chooses two cards from the face-up piles to get information about, and places them in a row *below* the secret cards. *A* places one green token alongside this row for each card in it that has the same rank *and* position as in *A*'a code, and one red token for each card in it that has just the same rank as in *A*'s code. The game continues, with *B* choosing further rows and *A* giving information, until *B* finds out the ranks and positions of the two secret cards.

*Scoring:* A (the code-maker) receives one token for each face-up row needed. Play three, five, or ten rounds. The player with more tokens wins.

## D 5–2 (ML)
Same as D 5–1, but A chooses *three*, instead of two, secret cards.

## D 5–3 (ML)
Same as D 5–1, but A chooses *four*, instead of two, secret cards, and use the 1–6, instead of 1–5, from both decks.

## D 5–4 (HL)
Same as D 5–1, but A chooses *five*, instead of two, secret cards, and use the 1–8, instead of 1–5, from both decks.

---

*Remark:* The code-maker gets more points for giving more information. It's best for the code-breaker to find out the secret cards by using as few rows as possible.

### Duplication Allowed
The players may agree before the game to allow the possibility that two (or more) secret cards have the same rank. Then, instead of placing cards face down to indicate the code, the code-maker writes down what the secret cards are on a piece of paper, which the code-breaker doesn't see.

This certainly makes the game more complicated than before. Let's look at some examples of codes and first trials for D 5–1, two out of five (LL), before we go through some complete games.

| | | |
|---|---|---|
| *Code:* | 1,2 | |
| *First Trial:* | 3,2 | G |

The green token shows that a 2 is in the same position in both the code and the first trial.

| | | |
|---|---|---|
| *Code:* | 1,2 | |
| *First Trial:* | 2,3 | R |

The red token here shows that a 2 is both in the code and in the first trial, but in different positions.

| | |
|---|---|
| *Code:* | 1,2 |
| *First Trial:* | 3,5 |

There are no tokens here because *neither* first trial card is in the code.

| | | | |
|---|---|---|---|
| *Code:* | 1,2 | | |
| *First Trial:* | 2,1 | R | R |

The two red tokens here show that a 1 and a 2 are both in the code and in the first trial, but in different positions.

The possible outcomes for *any* trial are:

- two green tokens,
- two red tokens,
- one green token,
- one red token, or
- no token.

You cannot have an outcome of one green and one red token. Do you see why? Such an outcome would mean that one card in that trial was in the code and in the right position, and that "another" card in that trial was in the code but *not* in the right position. But this "other" card could be in no other position.

Remember that the outcome "no token" means that neither card in the trial is also in the code. It does *not* mean "no information." In fact, a "no-token" outcome often gives you more information than a one-token outcome.

Let's now look at some examples of codes and first trials for D 5–2, three out of five (ML).

| | | |
|---|---|---|
| Code: | 1,4,2 | |
| First Trial: | 1,5,3 | G |

Here the green token shows there is a 1 in both the code and in the first trial, in the same position (on the left) in each.

| | | |
|---|---|---|
| Code: | 1,4,2 | |
| First Trial: | 3,5,1 | G |

Here the red token shows there is a 1 in both the code and in the first trial, but on the left in one case and on the right in the other.

| | | |
|---|---|---|
| Code: | 1,4,2 | |
| First Trial: | 4,3,1 | R R |

Here two red tokens show that there are a 4 and a 1 in both the code and in the first trial, but they are not in the same positions.

| | | |
|---|---|---|
| Code: | 1,4,2 | |
| First Trial: | 4,3,2 | G R |

Here the one green and one red token show that the 4 and 2 are in both the code and the first trial, but only the 2 is in the same position (on the right).

| | | |
|---|---|---|
| Code: | 1,4,2 | |
| First Trial: | 4,1,2 | G R R |

Here the one green and two red tokens show that all three code cards are in the first trial, but only the 2 is in the same position.

Let's now look at a sample game of D 5–3, 4 out of 6, *no duplication allowed* (ML):

| | | |
|---|---|---|
| First Trial: | 1,2,3,4 | G G R |

On the first trial we have located two of the cards in the code in their correct positions, and a third card in the code in the wrong position. We can now analyze exactly what all the possible codes are.

Let's begin by seeing which two cards in the first trial might be in the correct positions in the code. There are six different possibilities:

- 1 and 2,
- 1 and 3,
- 1 and 4,

- 2 and 3,
- 2 and 4, and
- 3 and 4.

For each of these possibilities, either the 5 or the 6 could be the code card *not* in the first trial, and it could be in either of two positions. All together, then, after the first trial, there are 24 possibilities for what the secret code is:

|  | 1 2 − − | 1 − 3 − | 1 − − 4 | − 2 3 − | − 2 − 4 | − − 3 4 |
|---|---|---|---|---|---|---|
| If 5 is also | 1 2 5 3 | 1 5 3 2 | 1 5 2 4 | 5 2 3 1 | 5 2 1 4 | 5 1 3 4 |
| in the code | 1 2 4 5 | 1 4 3 5 | 1 3 5 4 | 4 2 3 5 | 3 2 5 4 | 2 5 3 4 |
| If 6 is also | 1 2 6 3 | 1 6 3 2 | 1 6 2 4 | 6 2 3 1 | 6 2 1 4 | 6 1 3 4 |
| in the code | 1 2 4 6 | 1 4 3 6 | 1 3 6 4 | 4 2 3 6 | 3 2 6 4 | 2 6 3 4 |

Suppose on the second trial, that we keep the 3 and 4 in the same positions, move the 2 to where the 1 was, and add the 5 instead of the 1.

*Second Trial:* 2,5,3,4   G   R

On this trial, two cards are in the code, one in the correct position, and one not. Since on the first trial, *three* cards were in the code, the card we dropped, (the 1) must be in the code, and the card we added (the 5), must *not* be in the code. Since we knew from the first trial that either the 5 or the 6 must be in the code, and now we know the 5 isn't in it, then the 6 must be.

The code contains a 1 and a 6. Nine of the 24 possible we were left with after the first trial contain a 1 and a 6:

| | | | | | |
|---|---|---|---|---|---|
| 1 2 6 3 | 1 6 3 2 | 1 6 2 4 | 6 2 3 1 | 6 2 1 4 | 6 1 3 4 |
| 1 2 4 6 | 1 4 3 6 | 1 3 6 4 | | | |

But only six of these nine are consistent with the new information from the second trial: one card in the correct position, and one in the wrong position:

| | | | |
|---|---|---|---|
| 1 6 3 2 | 1 6 2 4 | 6 2 3 1 | 6 2 1 4 |
| 1 4 3 6 | 1 3 6 4 | | |

On our third trial let's try one of these six possibilities.

*Third Trial:*    1,6,3,2    G    G    R

We see we have three cards in the code: two in correct positions and one in a wrong position. Just two of the six possible codes fit this result: 1,4,3,6 and 1,6,2,4. We'll try the first.

*Fourth Trial:*    1,4,3,6    G    G    G    G

We've got it! In this case we needed four trials to find out the code. Let's explore some other trials we might have tried, and see what the results would have been.

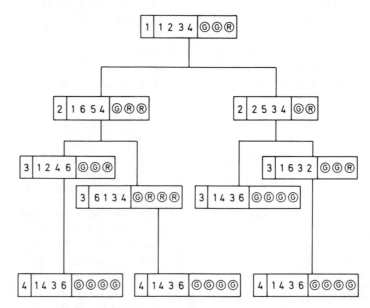

The preceding "tree diagram" starts with our actual first trial: 1,2,3,4. It shows two main branches for the second trial, 1,6,5,4, which we didn't take, and 2,5,3,4, which we did. For each of these possible second trials, it shows two possible third trials. Notice that by *luck* we might have found the secret code in just three trials.

This diagram shows only *some* of the paths we might have taken, and what the results would have been.

Let's look next at a sample game of D 5–4, five out of eight, duplication *allowed* (HL). Here are the results of five trials:

| | | | | |
|---|---|---|---|---|
| *First Trial:* | 1,2,3,4,5 | R R R | | |
| *Second Trial:* | 6,6,6,7,7, | | | |
| *Third Trial:* | 8,2,4,1,2 | R R R | | |
| *Fourth Trial:* | 2,8,2,5,5 | G G R R | | |
| *Fifth Trial:* | 2,5,2,8,4 | G G G G | | |

From the second trial, we know that 6 and 7 are not in the code. What two cards *are* in the correct positions in the fourth trial? Neither the 8 nor either 5, because in trial five the 8 and 5 are in changed positions and the number of cards in correct positions *increases* from two to four. So the two 2s must be in the correct positions in the fourth trial. The code must be 2,–,2,–,–.

Since four of the cards in trial four are in the code, at least one code card is a 5. From the fifth trial we know the position of the 5 in the code. So the code must be 2,5,2,–,–. We now know three of the four cards that are in the correct positions in (5).

What is the other? It can be only the 8 or the 4. If it were the 4, then the 8 is not in the code. If the 8 is not in the code, then trial four tells us that there are two 5s in the code. We already know that one 5 is in the code: 2,5,2,–,–. The other one would have to be in the fourth or fifth position, and we know from the fourth trial that this can't be: The two cards in the correct positions in that trial are the two 2s. So the 8 must be in the correct position in trial four. The code must be 2,5,2,8,–.

What is the last card in the code? It can't be a 1 or a 4, because the three code cards in trial three are 8, 2, and 2. Look now at the first trial, which contains three code cards. Two are the 2 and the 5. Since 1 and 4 are not in the code, the 3 must be the other code card in trial one. The complete secret code is therefore 2,5,2,8,3.

This group of games, D 5, is a most important one for exercising and strengthening your deductive logic muscle. We have analyzed for you at least one sample game for each game in the group. Now find a comfortable and enjoyable level to play at in this group, master that level, and move forward!

## RANKS AND POSITIONS BY TURNING CARDS AT RANDOM

Once again, you have to find the ranks and positions of the secret cards. But, instead of choosing which cards you want to get information about, they are chosen at random for you.

---

## D 6–1 (LL)
### RULES OF THE GAME

*Aim of the Game*: To find the code (*ranks* and *positions*) of some out of many (three out of five) secret cards by turning cards up at random to get information.

*Number of Players*: Two

*Materials Needed*: The aces through 5s (1–5) from both decks; green and red tokens.

| | | | | |
|---|---|---|---|---|
| The code | ⬛ ⬜ ⬛ | | | |
| First row | 1  4  3 | (R) | | Red token |
| Second row | 2  3  5 | (G) (G) | | Green token |

*How to Play*: *A* (as *code-maker*) chooses three cards of different ranks to be the secret cards (the cards in the *code*), and places them face down on the table without *B* seeing what they are. *A* then places the top three cards from the shuffled deck, face up and in a row, *below* the secret cards. These are the cards *A* will give information about. *A* places one green token alongside this row for each card in it that has the same rank *and* position as in *A*'s code, and one red token for each card in it that has just the same rank as in *A*'s code. The game continues, with *A* dealing out further rows at random and giving *B* information, until *B* finds out the code.

*Scoring*: *A* (the code-maker) receives one token for each face-up row needed. After each player has had an equal number of times in each role, the player with more tokens wins.

## D 6–2 (ML)
Same as D 6–1, but *A* chooses *four*, not three, secret cards, and use 1–6 from both decks.

## D 6–3 (HL)
Same as D 6–1, but *A* chooses *five*, not three secret cards, and use 1–8 from both decks.

# RANKS AND POSITIONS AMONG FOUR PLAYERS

In the next game, instead of one player giving out information and the other player(s) doing the thinking, the responsibility for giving out information is shared among four people. Each person knows the rank and position of one secret card, and each tries to figure out the ranks and positions of all four secret cards.

## D 7 (HL)
### RULES OF THE GAME

*Aim of the Game*: To find the code (ranks and positions) of the four secret cards by getting information from the other three players.

*Number of Players*: Four

*Materials Needed*: The aces through 6s (1–6) of both decks; green and red tokens; pencil and paper; grid 8 ×5.

*Preparation*: The 1–6 of spades are shuffled together. Each player takes one of these cards without letting the other players see it. This is the player's secret card. Only its rank is important.

The 1–5 of hearts are shuffled together. Each player takes one of these cards without letting the other players see it. This indicates the *position* of the player's secret card. a 1 means grid position 1, a 2 means grid position 2, and so on. With four players and five positions, one position will be empty. No one sees the card telling which position will be empty.

Each player writes down on a piece of paper kept hidden from the others what his or her secret card is and what position it goes into. All the cards are returned to the deck.

*How to Play*: Player A chooses any four cards of different ranks and places them face up, one card to a square in the top row of the grid. One square in the row remains empty. Players B, C, and D each place a green token, a red token, or nothing next to the row.

1. A green token indicates that the player's secret card is in the correct position in A's row.

2. A red token means the player's secret card is in a wrong position in A's row.

3. Nothing shows that the player's secret card is not in *A*'s row.

Then player *B* lays down a row of four cards, and players *A*, *C*, and *D* respond with the appropriate tokens. Play continues in rotation in this way.

A player who thinks he or she has figured out the code shouts out, "I've got it!" Play stops, and that player lays out a row of cards to show the solution. If correct, that player wins. If wrong, that player has lost but must continue in the game to give information to the other players about his or her secret card.

## D 7–2 (HL)
Use cards 1 through 10, instead of 1 through 6.

Let's see how this game might go. Suppose this is the code:

| 6 | | 1 | 3 | 4 |
|---|---|---|---|---|
| B | | D | A | C |

Below each square we show which player, *A*, *B*, *C*, or *D*, knows the rank of the card in it. *A* begins by laying down this row:

| 6 | 5 | 3 | 1 | | Ⓖ | Ⓡ |
|---|---|---|---|---|---|---|

*A* knows, of course, that a 3, not a 1, belongs in the fourth box, but *A* wants to confuse the other players. *B* puts down a green token, because the 6, *B*'s card, is in the correct position in *A*'s row. *C* puts down nothing, because the 4, *C*'s card, isn't in *A*'s row. *D* puts down a red token; the 1, *D*'s card, is in the wrong position in *A*'s row.

Each player will reach different conclusions from the information received. From *A*'s point of view, either the 6 or the 5 must be the card in the correct position indicated by the green token. The 3 cannot be, because it belongs in the fourth position. And the 1 can't be, because it is wrongly placed in the fourth position. If the 6 is in the correct position, then the 5 or the 1 is the card in the wrong position (indicated by the red token). If the 5 is in the correct position, then the 6 or the 1 is the card in the wrong position (indicated by the red token).

From *B*'s point of view, the 6 is in the correct position, and either the 5, 3, or 1 is in the wrong position. *A*'s card may also be in either the correct position or the wrong position in this row, or it may not be present at all.

From *C*'s point of view, either the 6, 5, 3, or 1 is in the correct position, and at least one of them is in the wrong position. *A*'s card may also be in either the correct position or the wrong position in this row, or it may not be present at all.

From *D*'s point of view, either the 6, 5, or 3 is in the correct position. *A*'s card may also be in the correct position or the wrong position in this row, or it may not be present at all.

As *B* now chooses a row and the other players respond, each player continues to narrow down the possibilities for what the secret code might be.

## RANKS, SUITS, AND POSITIONS BY CHOOSING CARDS

In this last group of games, you must find the suits of the cards in the secret code, in addition to their *ranks* and *positions*.

## D 8 (HL)
### RULES OF THE GAME

*Aim of the Game:* To find the rank, suit, and position of a code of three cards out of four by choosing what cards you want information about.

*Number of Players:* Two

*Materials Needed:* The aces through 4s (1–4) from both decks; pencil and paper; blue, green, and red tokens.

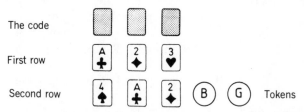

*How to Play: A* (as *code-maker*) chooses three cards of the deck and places them face down in a row on the table. This is *A*'s code. *B* (as *code-breaker*) selects any three cards to get information about and places them below *A*'s row. *A* gives *B* three kinds of information:

1. How many cards have the correct *rank* and *suit* in the correct position. For each, *A* puts down a *blue* token.

2. How many cards have *just* the correct *rank* in the correct position. For each, *A* puts down a *green* token.

3. How many cards have *just* the correct *suit* in the correct position. For each, *A* puts down a *red* token.

*B* writes this information down. The game continues until *B* finds out the ranks, suits, and positions of the code. Then the players switch roles and repeat the game.

*Scoring: A* gets one point for each trial needed. After each full round (each player with a turn as dealer), the player with the higher score is the winner.

---

*Remark:* The code-maker gets more points for giving more information. It's best for the code-breaker to find out the secret cards by using as few rows as possible.

Here's how a sample game might go, in which only three trials are needed to find rank, suit and order!

| | | How Many in Correct Positions | | | Possibilities | | | | | |
|---|---|---|---|---|---|---|---|---|---|---|
| | | R & S | R | S | Rank | | | Suit | | |
| | | | | | 1st Card | 2nd Card | 3rd Card | 1st Card | 2nd Card | 3rd Card |
| 1. | 1C, 2D, 3H | 0 | 0 | 0 | 234 | 134 | 124 | DHS | CHS | CDS |
| 2. | 4S, 1C, 2D | 1 | 1 | 0 | | | | | | |
| | If 4S in cp for R & S, then: | | | | 4 | 1 | 14 | S | HS | CS |
| | | | | or | 4 | 34 | 2 | S | HS | CS |
| | If 1C is in cp for R & S, then: | | | | 4 | 1 | 12 | DH | C | CS |
| | | | | or | 23 | 1 | 2 | DH | C | CS |
| | If 2D is in cp for R & S, then: | | | | 4 | 34 | 2 | DH | HS | D |
| | | | | or | 23 | 1 | 2 | DH | HS | D |
| 3. | 4S, 4H, 2S | 1 | 1 | 1 | 4 | 3 | 2 | S | H | C |

Here is how deductive logic is applied to the information from each trial:

1. The three cards in this row, from left to right, are the ace of clubs (1C), the 2 of diamonds (2D), and the 3 of hearts (3H). *None* has both rank and suit—just rank or just suit—in the correct position (cp). If the ace, in the left position, is not in the cp, then either a 2, 3, or 4 must be on the left in the code. In the same way, if a 2 is not in the correct position in the center, then the center card in the code must be a 1, 3, or 4. By the same reasoning, if a diamond is not in the cp in the center, then either a club, heart, or spade must be the center card in the code. This is the way the "Possibilities" were obtained for the first row.

2. In this row one card has its *rank* and *suit* in the correct position, and one card has only its rank in the correct position. We consider in turn each card as the one that might have both *rank* and *suit* in the cp, and look at what results must follow. For example, if the 4S had its rank and suit in the cp, then either the 1 or the 2 has its rank in the cp. Suppose the 1 does. Then we can eliminate possible ranks for the cards in the code.

|  | *Possibilities* | | |
|---|---|---|---|
|  | *1st Card* | *2nd Card* | *3rd Card* |
| After Row 1: | 234 | 134 | 124 |
| If 4S has its rank and suit in the cp: | 4 | 134 | 124 |
| And 1 has its rank in the cp: | 4 | 1 | 124 |
| But 2 cannot be on the right because it is not in the cp: | 4 | 1 | 14 |

In the same way we reached the other "Possibilities" for Row 2 through deductive reasoning.

3. Here one card has both rank and suit in the cp, one just its rank, and one just its suit. We consider each card in turn—the 4S, the 4H, and the 2S—as the card that might have both rank and suit in the cp, and look at what results must follow. If the 4S is that card, then we know from the last "Possibilities" that the possible ranks for the code are:

| *1st Card* | *2nd Card* | *3rd Card* |
|---|---|---|
| 4 | 1 | 14 |
| 4 | 34 | 2 |

We can eliminate 4,1,1 and 4,1,4, because, with either of them as the code cards, Row 3 would not have one card with just its rank in the cp. That leaves 4,3,2 and 4,4,2. But if the code cards were 4,4,2, then the information for the row would have been 1 2 0 not 1 1 1. So the three ranks must be 4,3,2. This means that the 2S is the card whose rank is in the cp but whose suit isn't. So the 4H must have its suit in the cp. The three suits must be S,H,C, and the code cards are 4S,3H,2C.

When we next try the 4H and then the 2S as the card that has both rank and suit in the correct position, we reach the same conclusion: the code cards are 4S,3H,2C.

We admit it's a bit complicated. But you see the *power* of deductive reasoning: With information from just *three* rows of cards, you can figure out the rank, suit, and position of all three cards in the code!

*Note:* In playing this game, you may not have enough of a certain card. For example, in our sample game, you need three 4Hs for the code, and for Rows 2 and 3. Yet, of course, only two 4Hs appear in two decks of cards. The solution is simple. You need paper and pencil in this game anyway to keep track of all the information and logical steps. As you get information about the cards you select for your Row 1, write down what the cards were and what the information was. Then reuse the cards for later rows as needed.

## APPLICATIONS

### 1

Six cards are face down. Two are jacks, two are queens, and two are kings. We have labeled them "A" through "F" to refer to them more easily. A "common border" exists between cards A and C, between B and C, between C and F, and so on.

1. Each jack shares a common border with a queen, and each queen shares a common border with a jack.
2. Each queen shares a common border with a king, and each king shares a common border with a queen.

Is card B a queen?

Does this situation remind you of any situations you met in the games of this chapter? Of the six face-down cards, you know that two each are jacks, queens, and kings, but you don't know which are which. In many of the games in this chapter, you knew "something" about the identity of face-down cards, but you didn't know which was which. For example, in the sample game D 5–4, these were the results of five trials:

*First Trial:*    1,2,3,4,5   (R) (R) (R)
*Second Trial:*   6,6,6,7,7,
*Third Trial:*    8,2,4,1,2   (R) (R) (R)
*Fourth Trial:*   2,8,2,5,5   (G) (G) (R) (R)
*Fifth Trial:*    2,5,2,8,4   (G) (G) (G) (G)

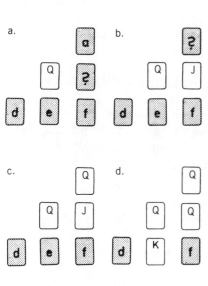

Each trial told you something about five face-down cards called the "secret code." Trial four told you that the row 2,8,2,5,5 had two cards in the same position as in the code, but it didn't tell you which they were. To find out, we looked at different possibilities. We said, for instance, "Suppose they are the 8 and a 5. Let's see if this fits with other information."

Here too we can look at different possibilities. If card B *is* a queen, how does this fit with other information? If card B were a queen, what could card C be? Since each queen shares a common border with a jack, and also shares a common border with a king, card C would have to be a jack or a king. (See layouts a & b.) Let's say card C is a jack. What then could card A be? Since card A has only one common border, shared with a jack, it would have to be a queen (See layout c.) But there are two kings, and each has to border on a queen, and only one of them can be card E. (See layout d.)

A similar argument applies if card B were a queen and card C a king. Then card A would have to be a queen. (See layouts e and f.) But there are two jacks and each has to border on a queen, and only one of them can be card E.

To summarize: If card B were a queen, then card C would have to be a jack or king. But card C cannot be a jack or king. So card B cannot be a queen.

If you see how to apply deductive logic here, then you can use the same principles in the next situation.

**2**

1. A, B, and C are three cards.

2. The sum of the ranks of cards A and B is 15.

3. The sum of the ranks of cards B and C is 17.

4. No card is a 7.

5. No card is higher than a 9.

6. What are the three cards?

Does this situation remind you of any situations you met in the games of this chapter? In our sample game of D 5–3, four out of six, we listed all 24 possible codes that fit the first piece of information we were given. Then, as we got more information, we were able to whittle down those 24 possibilities to 9, to 6, and eventually to 1.

Let's see if that approach works here. Of the four pieces of information that we have, let's begin with the piece of information that the sum of the ranks of cards A and B is 15. Here are the possibilities:

| A | B | | A | B |
|----|----|----|----|----|
| 13 | 2 | | 7 | 8 |
| 12 | 3 | | 6 | 9 |
| 11 | 4 | | 5 | 10 |
| 10 | 5 | | 4 | 11 |
| 9 | 6 | | 3 | 12 |
| 8 | 7 | | 2 | 13 |

We don't include 14 and 1, because no card has a rank higher than that of the king, 13. So we have 12 different possibilities for the ranks of cards A and B. We could now use our second piece of information, that the sum of the ranks of B and C is 17, to add a third column to our table:

| A | B | C | A | B | C |
|----|----|----|----|----|----|
| 13 | 2 | 15 | 7 | 8 | 9 |
| 12 | 3 | 14 | 6 | 9 | 8 |
| 11 | 4 | 13 | 5 | 10 | 7 |
| 10 | 5 | 12 | 4 | 11 | 6 |
| 9 | 6 | 11 | 3 | 12 | 5 |
| 8 | 7 | 10 | 2 | 13 | 4 |

We can eliminate our first two possibilities, because no card can be higher than 13. By taking into account that no card is a 7, we eliminate two more possibilities. Finally, since no card is higher than a 9, we eliminate all but one possibility: A=6, B=9, and C=8.

Do you think we would have gotten the same result by using our four pieces of information in a different order? Try it and see.

---

**3**

The four cards to the left are of four different ranks (an ace, king, queen, and jack) and of four different suits (clubs, diamonds, hearts, and spades), but not necessarily in that order.

1. The ace is in the upper left.
2. The spade is in the lower right.
3. The queen is in the upper right.
4. The king is the king of clubs.
5. The ace is not the ace of diamonds.

What is the rank and suit of each card in each location?

---

In some ways, this is like game D 4–1. We are given four cards, and we have to find out their positions.

Do you see how this situation is *different* from game D 4–1? A minor difference is that the cards are in a 2×2 arrangement, not in a row. A more important difference is that we must find out not only the position of the queen, for example, but also which queen it is. Another important difference is that, instead of being given just *one* kind of information (how many cards on each trial are in the correct positions), we are given several kinds of information (what rank is where, what suit is where, what rank goes with what suit, what rank doesn't go with that suit). We need, then, a *systematic* way to bring these different kinds of information together.

Let's see what we can do with the information we are given. We can use the first three facts directly. (See layouts a–c.) How can we now use the fact that the king is the king of clubs? Since the king can't be a spade, it must belong in the lower left. (See layout d.) And this means the jack must go in the lower right. (See layout e.

f. 

e.) Finally, if the ace is not the ace of diamonds, then it must be the ace of hearts (the only suit left), and therefore the queen is the queen of diamonds. (See layout f ).

**4**

Arthur, Bert, Charlie, and Dennis went into a store. One bought a watch, another a book, the third a pair of slippers, and the fourth a camera. The store has four floors. On each of the floors, only one kind of item is sold:

1. Arthur went to the first floor.

2. Watches are sold on the fourth floor.

3. Charlie went to the second floor.

4. Bert bought a book.

5. Arthur didn't buy a camera.

Who bought what where?

Do you see where this situation is similar not only to the last one but also to game D 4 −1? We can think of the men (Arthur, Bert, Charlie, Dennis) as four ranks (just like ace, 2, 3, 4). The things they bought (watch, book, slippers, camera) are equivalent to the four suits (just like clubs, diamonds, hearts, spades). And the four floors of the store are the four positions in a row. Then we can say the problem is the familiar one of finding out which card goes where. Once again, we are given several different kinds of information (who went where, what's sold where, what someone bought, what someone didn't buy).

And once again, it's important to find a *systematic* way to bring these different kinds of information together. We can begin with the diagram to the left that allows for all possibilities: *any* object might be sold to *any* man on *any* floor. Then we'll see which possibilities we can eliminate. Since Arthur went to the first floor, place him there on the diagram. Next, since watches are sold on the fourth floor, place an "X" in box 4W. This means that watches are *not* sold on the first, second, or third floors; so we place "Os" in 1W, 2W, and 3W. This also means that books, slippers, and cameras are *not* sold on the fourth floor; so we place Os in 4B, 4S, and 4C.

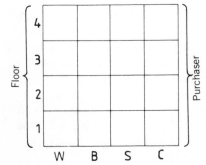

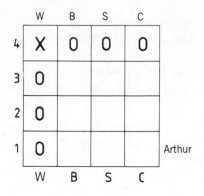

Next, we place Charlie on the second floor in the diagram, and consider the fact that Bert bought a book. Since Arthur and Charlie were on floors 1 and 2, Bert must have bought it on 3 or 4. But only watches are sold on the fourth floor, so Bert must have bought the book on the third. We place an X in 3B, Os in 1B, 2B, 3S and 3C, and Bert on the third.

|   | W | B | S | C |   |
|---|---|---|---|---|---|
| 4 | X | 0 | 0 | 0 |  |
| 3 | 0 | X | 0 | 0 | Bert |
| 2 | 0 | 0 |   |   | Charlie |
| 1 | 0 | 0 |   |   | Arthur |
|   | W | B | S | C |   |

Arthur didn't buy a camera. Looking at the diagram, we see he must have bought the slippers. We place an X in 1S, and Os in 2S and 1C. We see now that Charlie must have bought the camera, and Dennis made his purchases on the fourth floor.

|   | W | B | S | C |   |
|---|---|---|---|---|---|
| 4 | X | 0 | 0 | 0 | Dennis |
| 3 | 0 | X | 0 | 0 | Bert |
| 2 | 0 | 0 | 0 | X | Charlie |
| 1 | 0 | 0 | X | 0 | Arthur |
|   | W | B | S | C |   |

---

**5**

Ann, Betty, Carol, Diane, Eve, and Frances were six finalists in a beauty contest that was to have three winners.

1. *Modern Woman* magazine predicted that Betty would win first prize, Diane second prize, and Carol third prize.

2. *Glamorous Living* magazine predicted that Betty would win first prize, Frances second prize, and Ann third prize.

3. *Fashion and Family* magazine predicted that Ann would win first prize, Eve second prize, and Betty third prize.

It turned out that *Modern Woman* was right about just one of the winners and which prize she won; *Glamorous Living* was right about who two of the winners were but only got one of their prizes right; and *Fashion and Family* correctly named all three winners but wrongly predicted which prize each would get.

Who won each prize?

This situation is like a game of finding the rank and position of three out of six, with no duplication allowed. The "6" are finalists, instead of ace, 2, and so on. The "3" are the first, second, and third prize winners, instead of first, second, and third cards. Each magazine is like a row of cards about which you get information. We could arrange the information this way:

1. *Modern Woman*        B D C
2. *Glamorous Living*     B F A
3. *Fashion and Family*  A E B

From the last row we know that Ann, Eve, and Betty were all winners, but none was in that order. The first row winner must have been Betty, who won first prize. So Eve must have won third prize, and Ann second prize.

## 6

You have six coins that look alike. One of them is counterfeit and weighs more than each of the others. You also have a balance scale. In two weighings, how can you find out which coin is counterfeit?

This may seem like a strange situation, but is anything familiar about it? Does this situation remind you of any of the games in this chapter? In the "one out of many" games, D 1–1 through D 1–4, A chooses one card of many to be the secret card, and B must find it out by asking questions that have "yes" or "no" answers. In D 1–5, A chooses one person, place, or thing out of many, which B must find out by asking questions that have "yes" or "no" answers. In the present situation, one out of six coins has been "chosen," and you may ask two questions whose answers may be "heavier than," "equal to," or "lighter than." This situation is then not all that different from the games you have played.

Do you see how to apply principles learned from the games to this situation? One principle is to keep track of information in an organized way. Since the coins all look alike, let's begin by labeling them A, B, C, D, E, and F to tell them apart. For our first "question," put the same number of coins on each side of the balance scale. If one side is heavier, we know that the counterfeit coin is on that side. (This is like finding in game D 2 that one card on the first trial is in the code.) If the two sides weigh the same, we know that all the coins on the balance scale are genuine, and that the counterfeit one has been left off. (This is like getting *no* token in game D 2; you can learn a lot from this "negative" information.)

How many coins should we put on each side of the balance for our first question? One principle from the games is to list all possibilities. If we have six coins and want to put the same number of them on each side of the scale, the possibilities are 1, 2, or 3.

Suppose we choose 1, and place A against B. We will use a "tree diagram" (p. 52, top) to show our possible choices and outcomes, as we did for game D 5–3. If we are lucky, with just one weighing we may find that A is the counterfeit coin (outcome 1) or that B is the counterfeit (outcome 3). But if we get outcome 2, we need a second weighing. Again we could choose to weigh one against one. If we get outcome 4 or 6, we know which coin is counterfeit; but if we get outcome 5, we don't. So if we decide to weigh one coin against one on each trial, we can't be sure of solving the problem with two

First weighing

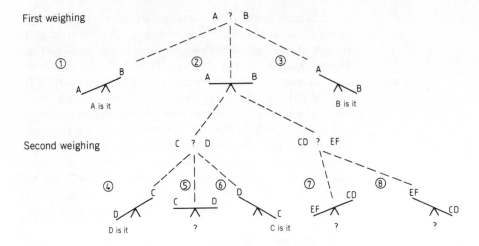

Second weighing

trials. We could alternatively weigh two against two on the second trial, getting either outcome 7 or outcome 8. In either case, we would *not* know which coin was counterfeit. To summarize, if we choose to weigh just one coin against another on the first trial, we cannot be sure of locating the counterfeit coin in two trials.

Let's look at two more tree diagrams to show you what could happen if we chose to weigh two against two or three against three on the first trial. We see that, if we begin with either two against two or with three against three on the first trial, it is always possible to find the counterfeit coin in two trials.

2 against 2

First weighing

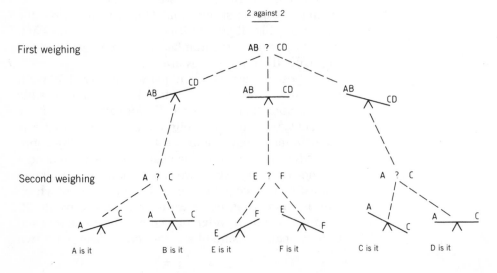

Second weighing

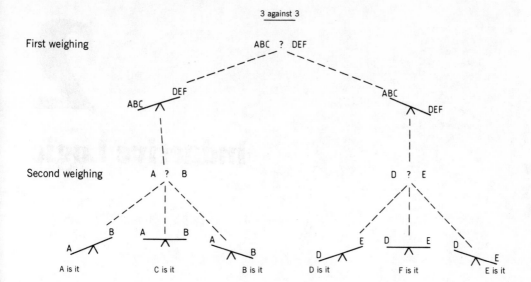

First weighing            ABC ? DEF

Second weighing

3 against 3

A is it        C is it        B is it        D is it        F is it        E is it

# 2

# Inductive Logic

The "rules" of nature tell us how things are: wood floats, magnets attract iron, and so on. There are also rules for operating effectively: avoid certain routes during rush hour, do not exercise strenuously right after eating, and the like. We have *rules* in so many aspects of our lives. Some rules are guides for *how* to do things, such as putting down the clutch before shifting gears. Other rules tell us what we are *supposed* to do, like stopping at a red light. Names are arranged in a telephone book according to *alphabetic* rules. The addresses of houses follow *numerical* rules: three houses in a row may be numbers 17, 19, and 21, but not 17, 21, and 19 or 17, 18, and 19. And they might be 17 Elm Street, 19 Elm Street, and 21 Elm Street, but not 17 Spruce Street, 19 Elm Street, and 21 Birch Street. These very simple rules we all take for granted.

We can discover these rules by putting our experiences together to see what is similar among different events. Doing so is called *induction*, that is, reasoning from particular facts to a general conclusion. We use induction very much in our daily lives, often without realizing it.

- I notice that, every day for a week, Harrington Road is very crowded going southbound in the early morning and going northbound in the late afternoon.

Through inductive reasoning, I avoid Harrington Road during these "rush" hours.

- If I play basketball after eating a heavy meal, I get a stomach ache; if I read, I don't. I notice these consequences a number of times. By inductive reasoning I tell myself to avoid strenuous exercise after eating.

- A shopper notices over several months that a supermarket is out of many items on Monday mornings.

- A baseball pitcher notices that a particular batter swings at very low pitches with two strikes against him.

- After seeing many films, a movie fan concludes that any movie with Jack Nicholson in it is a good one.

- A child notices that, whenever her father comes home from work and quickly has two drinks, he's in a bad mood.

- A student notices that one teacher calls on the students in the front row for answers very often, while another tends to call on students who sit near the window.

Scientists and people who develop new products use the same process of inductive logic to arrive at their rules as do shoppers, baseball pitchers, movie fans, and students to arrive at *their* rules. In this chapter we show you how to build your inductive reasoning ability by playing games. We will also show you how to apply inductive reasoning outside of the game settings to new situations and to your daily life.

The games in this chapter involve simple rules for regular changes in a row of cards. One player, the rule-maker, decides on a rule, and the other player, the rule-finder, must discover the rule. For example:

- Alternate diamonds and spades: first a diamond, then a spade, then a diamond, then a spade, and so on.

- Each card should be one higher than the last.

- Alternate diamonds and spades, and make each card one higher than the last.

Notice that a rule can involve the suit of a card, its rank, or both suit and rank.

Before we go further, you should know three terms that apply to all the groups of games in this chapter:

1. *Rank*: Each card has a number rank: ace=1, deuce=2, . . . ten=10, jack=11, queen=12, king=13.

2. *Number chain*: The ranks of the cards form an endless chain: 5, 6, 7, 8, 9, 10, jack, queen, king, ace, 2, 3, 4, 5, etc.

3. *Cycle*. A *cycle* is a complete set of changes that the rule calls for before the pattern repeats. For example, if a rule says "alternate diamonds and clubs," then a row of cards would be diamond, club, diamond, club, and so on. This would be a two-card cycle, that is, after two cards (diamond and club), the pattern repeats. Here are some other examples:

1. Two-card cycle   H, S, H, S . . .
2. Three-card cycle   C, D, H, C, D, H . . .
3. Three card cycle   C, D, D, C, D, D . . .
4. Four-card cycle   C, D, H, S, C, D, H, S . . .
5. Four-card cycle   C, H, H, S, C, H, H, S . . .

Remember to discuss each game with the other players when it is over, letting the rule-finders explain their thinking behind each choice. Everyone gets more out of the game by sharing their thoughts. You can learn both from your own mistakes and from the mistakes of others.

## FINDING THE RULE OF REGULAR CHANGE

### I 1–1 (LL)
**RULES OF THE GAME**

*Aim of the Game*: Given a row of cards, to find the rule of regular change in *suit and rank* (one change in each) and to find the specific card that comes next.

*Number of Players*: Two

*Materials Needed*: Deck of cards.

*How to Play*: A (as *rule-maker*) decides on a rule for regular change in a row of cards. The rule must repeat the same change in rank and the same change in suit from card to card, and it must indicate one specific card that comes next at each point. *A* places four cards face up in a row to illustrate the rule. *B* (as *rule-finder*) must guess what card comes next. *B* places the card that he or she thinks comes next at the end of the row and states the rule. If *B* has the right card and the right rule, *B* wins. If not, *A* removes the card, and puts the right card in its place. *B* continues with more trials until finding the rule. Then players switch roles.

*Scoring*: The rule-maker gets one point for each trial. It's better for the rule-finder to come up with the rule in fewer trials. The first player to get ten points wins.

### I 1–2 (ML)
Same as I 1–1, except each cycle contains *two* changes in rank, and *no* changes in suit. *A* sets up two complete cycles to illustrate the rule.

### I 1–3 (HL)
Same as I 1–1, except each cycle contains *two* changes in rank, and *one* change in suit. *A* sets up two complete cycles to illustrate the rule.

---

Here's a sample game for I 1–1: *A* as rule-maker decides that diamonds and spades will alternate and that each card will be two lower than the last. *A* sets up this row of four cards: QD, 10S, 8D, 6S . . . . *B* guesses that the 4 of spades comes next and is wrong. *B* notices that each card was two lower than the one before but doesn't notice that diamonds and spades alternate.

*A* adds the 4D to the row: QD, 10S, 8D, 6S, 4D . . . . *B* guesses 2S and is right. Since *B* made two guesses, the rule-maker gets two points.

Here now is a sample game for I 1–3: *A* decides to alternate two hearts and one diamond (repeat) for suit changes within each cycle, and to alternate one higher and two higher (repeat) for rank changes within each cycle. *A* sets up two complete cycles: 1H, 2H, 4D, 5H, 7H, 8D . . . .

*B* guesses 9H. *B* has noticed how the suit changes but, looking too quickly, thinks the rule says just "one higher" for rank. *A* adds 10H to the row: 1H, 2H, 4D,

5H, 7H, 8D, 10H .... Now *B* recognizes and correctly states the rule for rank as "one higher, two higher (repeat)" and places the JH next. Since it took two guesses, *A* gets two points.

## GENERAL RULE OF REGULAR CHANGE IN SUIT: CHANCE

In the last group of games, the rule-maker must always choose a rule that requires *one specific card* to come next at each point. A rule that ignored rank and said only that clubs and diamonds alternate would not be specific enough, because *any* club could follow a diamond. In this group of games, by contrast, the rules refer to *groups* of cards, not to specific cards. These games, although easy to play, are sometimes hard to understand when they are described. After we present the rules, we will give many examples to clarify how to play.

---

## I 2–1 (LL)
### RULES OF THE GAME

*Aim of the Game*: To find the general rule of regular change of suit, with a cycle of no more than three cards, by turning cards up in a random way.

*Number of Players*: Two or more.

*Materials Needed*: Deck of cards; pencil and paper.

*Preparation*: *A* (as *rule-maker*) writes down a rule of regular change that governs a series of cards. The rule must involve only the *suit* of the cards, and it must repeat after no more than three cards. For example, club, diamond, heart (repeat), or black, black, red (repeat). The rule must refer to *groups* of cards, not to individual cards. *A* also puts, face down in a pile, all the cards that illustrate two complete cycles of the rule. To begin the game with just two players, *A* turns up one card that follows the rule and hands the rest of the deck to *B*. With more than two players, *A* shuffles and deals out the rest of the deck face down to the other players.

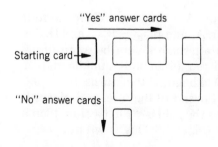

"Yes" answer cards

Starting card

"No" answer cards

*How to Play:* Each player in rotation turns up the top card of the pile. *A* tells each player whether that card *can* or *cannot* come next, according to the rule.

1. If it *can*, the player places it to the *right* of the first card (in a horizontal row).

2. If it *cannot*, the player places it *below* the last card turned up (in a vertical line).

The player then has a chance to state the rule.

1. If it is stated correctly, the game ends, and the next player becomes rule-maker.

2. If not, the player's turn ends, and the next player takes a card and continues.

The game continues until one player correctly states the rule. If no player has stated the rule correctly when all the cards have been turned up, the game ends, and next player becomes rule-maker. Play continues until each player has had the same number of turns as rule-maker.

*Scoring:*

1. *With two players:* The rule-finder gets one point for each card left in his or her hand when deal ends.

2. *With more than two players:* The player who correctly states the rule gets one point for each card remaining in all players' hands, including his or her own.

If no player has stated the rule correctly, the rule-maker gets 52 points. Scores are accumulated from deal to deal.

## I 2–2 (ML)

Same as I 2–1, except that the rule must repeat after no more than *four* cards, instead of three.

Here's how a game of I 2–1 might go: There are four players: the rule-maker, *A*, and players *B*, *C*, and *D*. *A*'s rule is that the cards alternate colors between *black* (clubs or spades) and *red* (diamonds and hearts). *A*  turns up the 3C (black) to begin. *B* then turns up the 9S, also black. *A* tells *B* it doesn't fit the rule, so *B* places it  *below* the 3C. *B* guesses the rule is, "First a club, then a diamond, then a heart (repeat)." This is wrong.

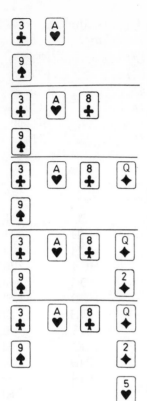

*C* then turns up the AH (red). *A* says it fits the rule, so *C* places it *to the right* of the 3C. *C* guesses, "Club, heart, spade, then repeat." This too is wrong. It is too specific: after a C, either a H or a D could come; after a H, either a C or S could come.

*D* then turns up the 8C. *A* says it fits the rule, so *D* places it to the right of the AH. *D*'s guess: "Club, heart, then repeat." Wrong.

*B* next turns up the QD. *A* says it fits the rule, so *B* places it *to the right* of the 8C. *B*'s guess is, "Club, heart, club, diamond, then repeat." Wrong. (This is a poor guess because a four-card cycle is not allowed in this game).

*C* then turns up the 2D (red). *A* says it doesn't fit the rule, so *C* places it *below* the QD. *C*'s guess: "Club, red card, then repeat." Wrong.

*D* then turns up the 5H. *A* says it does not fit the rule, and *D* places it below the 2D. *D* says, "I've got it. It's simple. Black, red, then repeat." *D* is correct, and the deal ends. *D* gets one point for each card remaining in each player's hand. *B* deals next.

Moral: Try the simple rules first.

In the discussion after the game, all the players explained their thinking behind their guesses. How did *D* figure out the rule? She noticed that the cards that didn't fit were always the same color as the last card that did fit: The 9S was the same color as the 3C, the 2D and 5H were the same color as the QD. All the players benefited from this discussion.

Is there a general method of figuring out the rule that *always* works? In the Deductive Logic chapter we learned it's sometimes useful to list all the possibilities and then, as new information comes in, eliminate those possibilities that don't fit with that information. In game I 2–1 the rule involves suit only, and it must repeat after either one, two, or three cards. So what are all the possibilities? There are 76 of them, grouped on the next page first by how long the cycle is, then listed alphabetically within each group.

Let's replay the same game, seeing what possibilities we can eliminate with each piece of information.

|  |  |
|---|---|
| *Repeats After* | *Repeats After* |
| *One Card* | *Two Cards* |

| | |
|---|---|
| C . . . | CD . . .    HC . . . |
| D . . . | CH . . .    HD . . . |
| H . . . | CS . . .    HS . . . |
| S . . . | DC . . .    SC . . . |
|  | DH . . .    SD . . . |
|  | DS . . .    SH . . . |

*Repeats After*
*Three Cards*

| | | | |
|---|---|---|---|
| CCD . . . | DCC . . . | HCC . . . | SCC . . . |
| CCH . . . | DCD . . . | HCD . . . | HCD . . . |
| CCS . . . | DCH . . . | HCH . . . | SCH . . . |
| CDC . . . | DCS . . . | HCS . . . | SCS . . . |
| CDD . . . | DDC . . . | HDC . . . | SDC . . . |
| CDH . . . | DDH . . . | HDD . . . | SDD . . . |
| CDS . . . | DDS . . . | HDH . . . | SDH . . . |
| CHC . . . | DHC . . . | HDS . . . | SDS . . . |
| CHD . . . | DHD . . . | HSC . . . | SHC . . . |
| CHH . . . | DHH . . . | HHD . . . | SHD . . . |
| CHS . . . | DHS . . . | HHS . . . | SHH . . . |
| CSC . . . | DSC . . . | HSC . . . | SHS . . . |
| CSD . . . | DSD . . . | HSD . . . | SSC . . . |
| CSH . . . | DSH . . . | HSH . . . | SSD . . . |
| CSS . . . | DSS . . . | HSS . . . | SSH . . . |

1. After the rule-maker positions the 3C as the first card that follows the rule, we can eliminate all rules that don't start with a club. Doing so leaves us:

| | | | |
|---|---|---|---|
| C . . . | CD . . . | CH . . . | CS . . . |
| CCD . . . | CCH . . . | CCS . . . | CDC . . . |
| CDD . . . | CDH . . . | CDS . . . | CHC . . . |
| CHD . . . | CHH . . . | CHS . . . | CSC . . . |
| CSD . . . | CSH . . . | CSS . . . |  |

2. The 9S doesn't come next, so we can eliminate all rules that begin CS. We are left with:

| | | | | |
|---|---|---|---|---|
| C . . . | CD . . . | CH . . . | CCD . . . | CCH . . . |
|  | CCS . . . | CDC . . . | CDD . . . | CDH . . . |
|  | CDS . . . | CHC . . . | CHD . . . | CHH . . . |
|  | CHS . . . |  |  |  |

3. After just two pieces of information, then, we are down from 76 original possibilities to just 14. We now find that the AH fits the rule, so we can eliminate those possibilities that don't begin CH. We are left with:

CH...     CHC...     CHD...     CHH...     CHS...

4. Now we are down to just five possibilities. We are told next that the 8C fits the rule, so we can eliminate any possibility that doesn't begin CHC. We are now down to just:

CH...     CHC...

Or are we? One possibility would have us predict a heart comes next: CH, CH .... The other possibility is a club: CHC, C .... But we discover that actually a *diamond* comes next according to the rule. What's going on here?

It's true that we were down to just two possibilities, CH (repeat) and CHC (repeat), but each possibility could mean several different things! CH (repeat) could really mean:

1. club, red card (repeat),
2. black card, heart (repeat),
3. black card, red card (repeat),
4. club or diamond, heart (repeat),
5. club or diamond, red card (repeat), and so on.

And CHC (repeat) could mean such things as:

1. club, heart, black card (repeat),
2. club, red card, club,
3. black card, diamond or heart, club (repeat), and the like.

We are not aware of all these possible meanings until after we see that the rules we are left with just didn't work.

From this example, you can see how you can use *deductive* logic as a powerful tool to eliminate possibilities, and how you can use *inductive* logic as a necessary tool to come up with new possibilities. In these games you must use *both*. At first by *induction* you think of a possible rule or of several possible rules—or of what you believe are *all* the possible rules. You get some information, and use *deduction* to eliminate possibilities. As you narrow down the possible rules, you may be forced to use *induction* again to generate new ones. When we were left with just two possible rules, and when neither correctly predicted the diamond that actually came next, we had to think of new possible rules to fit the information we had.

### GENERAL RULE OF REGULAR CHANGE IN SUIT: CHOICE

In the previous group of games, the cards you get information about come up at random. In the next game, you *select* the card you think will fit the rule.

---

### I 3–1 (ML)
#### RULES OF THE GAME

*Aim of the Game*: To find the general rule of a regular change of suit, with a cycle of no more than four cards, by selecting the cards to get information about.

*Number of Players*: Two or more.

*Materials Needed*: Deck of cards; pencil and paper.

*Preparation*: A (as *rule-maker*) writes down a rule of regular change that governs a series of cards. The rule must only involve the *suit* of the cards, and it must repeat after no more than four cards. For example, club, diamond, heart, spade (repeat), or three black, one red (repeat). The rule must refer to *groups* of cards, not to individual cards. A also puts, face down in a pile, cards that illustrate two complete cycles of the rule. If there are two players, A then turns up one card that follows the rule, to begin the play, and hands the rest of the deck to B. With more than two players, A shuffles and deals out the rest of the deck face down to the other players.

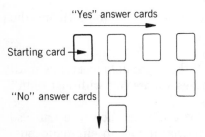

"Yes" answer cards

Starting card

"No" answer cards

*How to Play*: Each player in turn looks through and selects a card from his or her pile. *A* tells the player whether that card *can* or *cannot* come next, according to the rule.

1. If it *can*, the player places it to the *right* of the first card (in a horizontal row).
2. If it *cannot*, the player places it *below* the last card turned face up (in a vertical line).

The player then has a chance to state the rule.

1. If it is stated correctly, the game ends, and the next player becomes rule-maker.
2. If not, the player's turn ends, and the next player selects a card and continues.

A player can decline the chance to state the rule. A player who states the rule incorrectly must give up three cards, chosen at random, to *A*. A player who is out of cards loses.

The game continues until one player correctly states the rule. If no player has stated the rule correctly when all the cards have been turned up or when all the players are out of cards, the game ends, and next player becomes rule-maker. Play continues until each player has had the same number of turns as rule-maker.

*Scoring*:

1. *With two players*: The rule-finder gets one point for each card left in his or her hand when the deal ends.
2. *With more than two players*: The player who correctly states the rule gets one point for each card remaining in all players' hands, including his or her own.

If no player has stated the rule correctly, the rule-maker gets 52 points. Scores are accumulated from deal to deal.

---

## GENERAL RULE OF REGULAR CHANGE IN RANK: CHANCE

In the next game, the rule involves *rank*, instead of suit.

## I 4–1 (ML)
### RULES OF THE GAME

*Aim of the Game*: To find the general rule of regular change of rank, with a cycle of no more than four cards, by turning cards up in a random way.

*Number of Players*: Two or more.

*Materials Needed*: Deck of cards; pencil and paper.

*Preparation*: *A* (as *rule-maker*) writes down a rule of regular change that governs a series of cards. The rule must involve only the *rank* of the cards, and it must repeat after no more than four cards: for example, odd, odd, odd, even (repeat). The rule must refer to *groups* of cards, not to individual cards. *A* also puts, face down in a pile, cards that illustrate two complete cycles of the rule. To begin play with two players, *A* turns up one card that follows the rule and hands the rest of the deck to *B*. With more than two players, *A* shuffles and deals out the rest of the deck face down to the other players.

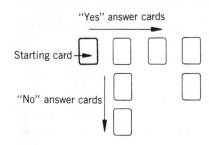

*How to Play*: Each player in rotation turns up the top card of the pile. *A* tells player whether that card *can* or *cannot* come next, according to the rule.

1. If it *can*, the player places it to the *right* of the first card (in a horizontal row).

2. If it *cannot*, the player places it *below* the last card turned face up (in a vertical line).

The player then has a chance to state the rule.

1. If it is stated correctly, the game ends, and the next player becomes rule-maker.

2. If not, the player's turn ends, and the next player takes a card and continues.

The game continues until one player correctly states the rule. If no player has stated the rule correctly when all the cards have been turned up, the game ends, and next player becomes rule-maker. Play continues until each player has had the same number of turns as rule-maker.

*Scoring*:

1. *With two players*: The rule-finder gets one point for each card left in his or her hand when the deal ends.

2. *With more than two players*: The player who correctly states the rule gets one point for each card remaining in all players' hands, including his or her own.

If no player has stated the rule correctly, the rule-maker gets 52 points. Scores are accumulated from deal to deal.

---

The arrangement below shows how a game might go when the dealer's rule is *7 or lower, 7 or lower, higher than 7*, (repeat).

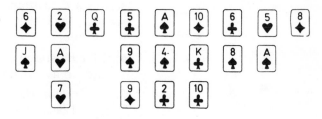

## GENERAL RULE OF REGULAR CHANGE IN RANK: CHOICE

The next game also involves rank rules, but in it you *select* the cards you want to get information about.

---

## I 5–1 (ML)
### RULES OF THE GAME

*Aim of the Game*: To find the general rule of regular change of rank, with a cycle of no more than four cards, by selecting the cards to get information about.

*Number of Players*: Two or more.

*Materials Needed*: Deck of cards; pencil and paper.

*Preparation*: A (as *rule-maker*) writes down a rule of regular change that governs a series of cards. The rule

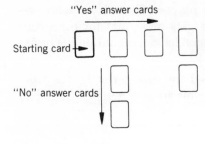

"Yes" answer cards

Starting card

"No" answer cards

must involve only the *rank* of the cards, and it must repeat after no more than four cards: for example, odd, odd, odd, even (repeat). The rule must refer to *groups* of cards, not to individual cards. *A* also puts, face down in a pile, cards that illustrate two complete cycles of the rule. To begin play with just two players, *A* turns up one card that follows the rule and hands the rest of the deck to *B*. With more than two players, *A* shuffles and deals out the rest of the deck face down to the other players.

*How to Play*: Each player in turn looks through and selects a card from his or her pile. *A* tells the player whether that card *can* or *cannot* come next, according to the rule.

1. If it *can*, the player places it to the *right* of the first card (in a horizontal row).
2. If it *cannot*, the player places it *below* the last card turned face up (in a vertical line).

The player then has a chance to state the rule.

1. If it is stated correctly, the game ends, and the next player becomes rule-maker.
2. If not, the player's turn ends, and the next player selects a card and continues.

A player can decline the chance to state the rule. A player who states the rule incorrectly must give up three cards, chosen at random, to *A*. A player who is out of cards loses.

The game continues until one player correctly states the rule. If no player has stated the rule correctly when all the cards have been turned up or when all the players are out of cards, the game ends, and the next player becomes rule-maker. Play continues until each player has had the same number of turns as rule-maker.

*Scoring*:

1. *With two players*: The rule-finder gets one point for each card left in his or her hand when the deal ends.
2. *With more than two players*: The player who correctly states the rule gets one point for each card remaining in all players' hands, including his or her own.

If no player has stated the rule correctly, the rule-maker gets 52 points. Scores are accumulated from deal to deal.

## GENERAL RULE OF REGULAR CHANGE IN RANK AND SUIT: CHANCE

In the last few games you have seen how to discover a rule that involves suit or that involves rank. The next game allows more complicated rules that involve both suit *and* rank.

### I 6–1 (HL)
#### RULES OF THE GAME

*Aim of the Game*: To find the general rule of regular change of suit and rank, with a cycle of no more than four cards, by turning cards up in a random way.

*Number of Players*: Two or more.

*Materials Needed*: Deck of cards; pencil and paper.

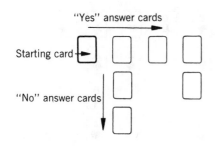

"Yes" answer cards

Starting card

"No" answer cards

*Preparation*: *A* (as *rule-maker*) writes down a rule of regular change that governs a series of cards. The rule may involve both the *suit* and the *rank* of the cards, and it must repeat after no more than four cards: for example, red, odd, black, even (repeat). The rule must refer to *groups* of cards, not to individual cards. *A* also puts, face down in a pile, cards that illustrate two complete cycles of the rule. To begin play with two players, *A* turns up one card that follows the rule and hands the rest of the deck to *B*. If there are more than two players, *A* shuffles and deals out the rest of the deck face down to the other players.

*How to Play*: Each player in rotation turns up the top card of the pile. *A* tells the player whether that card *can* or *cannot* come next, according to the rule.

1. If it *can*, the player places it to the *right* of the first card (in a horizontal row).

2. If it *cannot*, the player places it *below* the last card turned face up (in a vertical line).

The player then has a chance to state the rule.

1. If it is stated correctly, the game ends, and the next player becomes rule-maker.

2. If not, the player's turn ends, and the next player takes a card and continues.

The game continues until one player correctly states the rule. If no player has stated the rule correctly when all the cards have been turned up, the game ends, and next player becomes rule-maker. Play continues until each player has had the same number of turns as rule-maker.

*Scoring:* 
1. *With two players:* The rule-finder gets one point for each card left in his or her hand when the deal ends.

2. *With more than two players:* The player who correctly states the rule gets one point for each card remaining in all players' hands, including his or her own.

If no player has stated the rule correctly, the rule-maker gets 52 points. Scores are accumulated from deal to deal.

---

Here is an example. Can you figure out the rule?

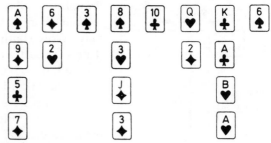

The solution is black, even (repeat).

**GENERAL RULE OF REGULAR CHANGE IN RANK AND SUIT: CHOICE**

---

## I 7–1 (HL)
**RULES OF THE GAME**

*Aim of the Game:* To find the general rule of regular change of suit and rank, with a cycle of no more than four cards, by selecting the cards to get information about.

*Number of Players:* Two or more.

*Materials Needed*: Deck of cards; pencil and paper.

*Preparation*: *A* (as *rule-maker*) writes down a rule of regular change that governs a series of cards. The rule may involve both the *suit* and the *rank* of the cards, and it must repeat after no more than four cards: for example, red, odd, black, even (repeat). The rule must refer to *groups* of cards, not to individual cards. *A* also puts, face down in a pile, cards that illustrate two complete cycles of the rule. To begin play with two players, *A* turns up one card that follows the rule and hands the rest of the deck to *B*. If there are more than two players, *A* shuffles and deals out the rest of the deck face down to the other players.

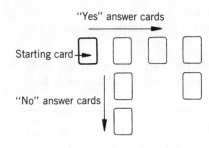

"Yes" answer cards

Starting card

"No" answer cards

*How to Play*: Each player in turn looks through and selects a card from his or her pile. *A* tells the player whether that card *can* or *cannot* come next, according to the rule.

1. If it *can*, the player places it to the *right* of the first card (in a horizontal row).
2. If it *cannot*, the player places it *below* the last card turned face up (in a vertical line).

Player then has a chance to state the rule.

1. If it is stated correctly, the game ends, and the next player becomes rule-maker.
2. If not, the player's turn ends, and the next player selects a card and continues.

A player can decline the chance to state the rule. A player who states the rule incorrectly must give up three cards, chosen at random, to *A*. A player who is out of cards loses.

The game continues until one player correctly states the rule. If no player has stated the rule correctly by the time that all the cards have been turned up or all the players are out of cards, the game ends, and next player becomes rule-maker. Play continues until each player has had the same number of turns as rule-maker.

*Scoring*:

1. *With two players*: The rule-finder gets one point for each card left in his or her hand when the deal ends.

2. *With more than two players*: The player who correctly states the rule gets one point for each card remaining in all players' hands, including his or her own.

If no player has stated the rule correctly, the rule-maker gets 52 points. Scores are accumulated from deal to deal.

---

*Rank* may make a difference in two different ways in the same rule. For example, let's look at the rule *even, seven or lower, odd, higher than seven*, (repeat). In this rule, whether a card is even or odd, and seven or lower, or higher than seven is important. And both considerations are based on rank.

These two ways that rank makes a difference could also be combined with the consideration of *suit* in the same rule: for example, *even, seven or lower, red*, (repeat).

A rule with *three* things that make a difference can be very hard to discover. And if you are looking for a rule with three things that make a difference, and in the actual rule only one thing makes a difference, such as *red, black*, (repeat), this otherwise very simple rule will be very hard for you. For this reason, we present the following variations:

*Variation 1.* Players agree beforehand that, in the rule, rank will make a difference in only one way, but don't say how.

*Variation 2.* Players agree beforehand that, in the rule, rank will make a difference in exactly two ways, but don't say how.

*Variation 3.* Players agree beforehand that, in the rule, rank may not make a difference, or it may make a difference in one or in two ways.

The next example involves a "special" rule in which both suit and rank make a difference.

| 9H | 9C | 7C | 3C | 2C | 2D | 9D | 6D | 6S | 7S | 7H | QH |
|----|-----|----|----|----|----|----|----|----|----|----|----|
| 10C | 10H | AH | 4D | 4S | JS | AC | 8C | | | 5C | |
| KD | AS | 8S | JD | 3D | 8H | | | | | | |
| 3S | | | 5S | | | | | | | | |
| 10S | | | 6H | | | | | | | | |
| 7S | | | 9S | | | | | | | | |
| | | | 5D | | | | | | | | |

The solution is that each card must either be of the same suit or have the same rank of the previous card.

## APPLICATIONS

We have given you many examples of possible rules. Use them. Try different combinations, and make up new kinds of rules we haven't mentioned. In playing the games in this chapter, you can learn a number of principles in inductive thinking:

- Try simple rules first.
- Get more information.
- List possibilities.
- Eliminate possibilities.
- Go back and forth between inductive and deductive logic.
- The "same" event may have more than one meaning.
- Pay attention to *all* changes from one "similar" event to another.
- See what things that *don't* fit a rule have in common.
- The same characteristics may make a difference in two different ways.
- Look for a *cycle*, which is a complete set of changes before a pattern repeats.

Now we will show you first how to apply these principles in a series of different, puzzle-like situations and then how to apply them in your daily life.

### Intelligence Test Questions
Induction is a thinking ability that appears frequently on intelligence tests. Here are some examples of intelligence test questions that are related to the games in this chapter. For each question, think about what game it may be related to and about what principles you have learned that you can apply.

---

**1**

*What comes next: 1, 3, 4, 6, 7, ?*

---

Does this remind you of any game in the chapter? In I 1–3 the goal was to find the rule of regular change and to find the card that came next. Our sample game had this row:

1H   2H   4D   5H   7H   8D . . .   ?

Our intelligence test question is very similar, but we don't have the distraction of *suit*; we just have a row of numbers.

To see what comes next, we must find the cycle, that is, the complete set of changes before the pattern repeats. We see it goes *two higher, one higher, two higher, one higher* . . . . The cycle is *two higher, one higher,* (repeat). The question mark comes after two complete cycles, so we add two and get *nine* as the answer.

---

**2**

What is missing from the diagram on the left?

Here there is one rule for going from left to right; it is a regular change from small to medium to large. Another rule applies for going from top to bottom; it is a regular change from square to circle to triangle.

---

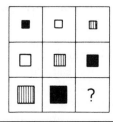

**3**

What is missing from the diagram?

The rule for going from top to bottom is easy: regular change from small to medium to large. But what is the rule for going from left to right? When we were looking at all possibilities for the rule in the same pages of

I 2–1, at one point we came down to just two possible rules. Neither one predicted what actually came next. At that point we began to look at things in a new way. We decided that a heart was a red card as well as a heart and that a club was a black card as well as a club.

Is there some way of looking at things in a new way here, so we can find a rule for going from left to right in the grid? Our usual way of looking at the first row (black, white, striped) is to take it as a model of what the other rows should be. Let's try the opposite possibility: the first row is a model for what the other rows *shouldn't* be. So the second row should *not* be black, white, striped. But what then should it be? Let's list the possibilities.

B  S  W
S  B  W
S  W  B
W  B  S
W  S  B

Of these possibilities, SBW and WSB are *completely* different from the first row: Each shading is in a different position than it is in the first row. If BSW is the model for what the other rows *shouldn't* be, then SBW could be one other row and WSB the other. Since we already know that WSB is the second row, SBW must be the third row, and large white square is missing. Thus, we have to go back and forth between *inductive* and *deductive* logic.

To summarize, the rule for going from top to bottom is regular change from small to medium to large. The rule for going from left to right is make each row as different as possible from the others. Another way to state this second rule is to have each kind of shading appear in a *different* position in each row.

---

**4**

These shapes fit the rule:

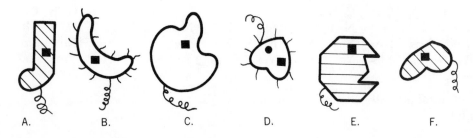

A.        B.        C.        D.        E.        F.

These shapes do *not* fit the rule:

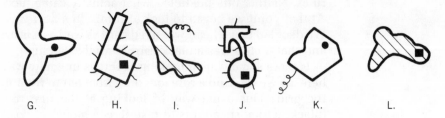

G.        H.        I.        J.        K.        L.

What is the rule?

Here the simple rules don't seem to work. Let's look at how each figure is the same or different from the others, and list the characteristics that might go into the rule:

1. Some have curly "tails," and some don't.
2. Some are made of curved lines, others of straight lines, others of both.
3. Some are shaded horizontally, some are shaded on a slant, and some aren't shaded.
4. Some have "hair," and some don't.
5. Some have small "objects" inside them, and some don't.

We will make a chart to see if any one characteristic or any combination of them can separate out those figures that fit the rule from those that don't.

| | Figures That Fit Rule | | | | | | Figures That Don't | | | | | |
|---|---|---|---|---|---|---|---|---|---|---|---|---|
| | A | B | C | D | E | F | G | H | I | J | K | L |
| 1. Tail? | Yes | Yes | Yes | Yes | Yes | Yes | No | No | Yes | No | Yes | No |
| 2. Line: | C+S | C | C | C | S | C | C | S | C | C+S | C+S | C |
| 3. Shading: | Slt | N | N | N | H | Slt | N | N | Slt | N | N | Slt |
| 4. Hair? | No | Yes | No | Yes | No | No | No | Yes | No | Yes | No | No |
| 5. Object inside? | Yes | Yes | Yes | Yes | Yes | Yes | Yes | Yes | No | Yes | Yes | Yes |

C=curved; S=straight; Slt=slanted; N=none; H=horizontal

There does not seem to be any way to tell from these characteristics whether or not a figure fits the rule. All the figures that fit the rule have tails and objects inside, but so does figure k, which doesn't fit the rule. We are at the same point as in the sample game of I 2–1, when we were left with just two possible rules, neither of which correctly predicted the card that actually came next. In that game, we had to think of new possible rules that fit the information we had.

So what other characteristics of these figures might make a difference? (Once again, we are going back and forth from inductive to deductive logic.) Here are some possibilities: the height of the figures, their areas, whether they are symmetrical, how many "hairs" they have, how long their "tails" are. Check these out.

We can apply another principle here: The "same" event may have more than one meaning. Remember that a heart is a red card as well as a heart. Do you see how to apply this principle? All the figures (except figure I) have "objects" inside, but there are two different kinds of objects, squares and circles. We can make each kind of object a separate entry in our chart:

| | *Figures That Fit Rule* | | | | | | *Figures That Don't* | | | | | |
|---|---|---|---|---|---|---|---|---|---|---|---|---|
| | *A* | *B* | *C* | *D* | *E* | *F* | *G* | *H* | *I* | *J* | *K* | *L* |
| 1. Tail? | Yes | Yes | Yes | Yes | Yes | Yes | No | No | Yes | No | Yes | No |
| 2. Line: | C+S | C | C | C | S | C | C | S | C | C+S | C+S | C |
| 3. Shading: | Slt | N | N | N | H | Slt | N | N | Slt | N | N | S |
| 4. Hair? | No | Yes | No | Yes | No | No | No | Yes | No | Yes | No | No |
| 5. Square inside? | Yes | Yes | Yes | Yes | Yes | Yes | No | Yes | No | Yes | No | Yes |
| 6. Circle inside? | No | No | No | Yes | No | No | Yes | No | No | No | Yes | No |

We see that all the figures that fit the rule have both "tails" and a square object inside, while none of the figures that don't fit the rule have both of these features. So the rule is that a figure must have both a tail and a square object inside.

We solved this problem by trying simple rules first, getting more information, listing possibilities, eliminating possibilities, going back and forth between *inductive* and *deductive* logic, and remembering that the "same" event (in this case, a small object inside) may have more than one meaning.

**Party Games**

The last application dealt with rules for which objects belong in a category and which objects do not. You can play a simple party game to increase your skill in finding such rules:

---

**5**

The aim of the game is to discover the leader's rule for what objects may be taken on a trip. The leader decides on and writes down a rule for what objects may be taken on a trip. The leader begins by saying, "I am going on a trip and I'm taking along a ——— [an object that the rule allows leader to take along]." The players alternate turns, asking, "May I take a ——— [naming an object they want information about]?" The leader answers each question "yes" or "no." A player who gets a "yes" answer is entitled to a guess as to what the rule is.

---

For example, the leader (L) is playing with players A, B, and C. L begins by saying, "I am going on a trip and I am taking a *newspaper*."

A: May I take a radio?

L: No.

B: May I take a frisbee?

L: No.

C: May I take a book?

L: Yes.

C: I think the rule is that you can take things to read.

L: No, that isn't it.

A: May I take a magazine?

L: Yes.

A: I think the rule is you can take along reading material that comes out on a regular basis.

L: No, that isn't it.

B: May I take an advertising circular?

L: Yes.

B: I think you can take anything with ads in it.

L: No, that isn't it.

C: May I take wrapping paper?

L: Yes.

C: I think the rule is you can take anything made out of paper.

L: You're right.

Now that we've seen how to increase and exercise your skill in inductive logic by playing a party game, let's see how that skill can be applied in science. This is an area in which inductive thinking is most important.

---

**6**

How could you find the rule that states which objects are attracted by a magnet and which objects aren't?

---

You could check whether a magnet attracts newspapers, shirts, nails, pennies, nickels, paper clips, pencils, oranges, needles, noodles, tin cans, and refrigerator doors. You might divide the objects up into Attracted and Nonattracted groups like this:

| *Attracted* | *Nonattracted* |
|---|---|
| nails | newspapers |
| paper clips | shirts |
| needles | pennies |
| tin cans | nickels |
| refrigerator doors | pencils |
| | oranges |
| | noodles |

(Actually, 1943 pennies are attracted by magnets.)

You may notice that all the attracted objects are made of metal, although a couple of nonattracted objects (pennies and nickels) are too. This might suggest to you that objects made out of just *certain* metals are attracted to magnets. You could check out this observations by testing more objects, some made out of the metals you think are attracted by magnets, and others made out of metals you think aren't.

This is like asking the dealer whether certain cards fit the rule—"Can a club come next?" or "Does a card higher than a seven belong here?"

# 3

# Strategy Games
# of Movement

Introduction to the Skill

*Game Number*
*and Level*

Strategy deals with making general plans to reach your goal. In olden times, if you didn't have the money to buy something, you saved money until you had enough, and then you bought it. *Saving* and then *buying* made up your strategy. A more recent strategy is to *borrow* the money and then to *buy* what you want. Can you think of other possible strategies to get what you want when you don't have the money for it? Let's list these two and other possible strategies:

- Save money, then buy what you want.
- Borrow money, then buy what you want.
- You could trade something you already have for what you want.
- You could borrow the item you want.
- You could rent what you want.

How could you divide these strategies into groups? Here's one way:

| *One-Stage Strategies* | *Two-Stage Strategies* |
| --- | --- |
| Trade for what you want. | Save money, then buy what you want. |
| Borrow what you want. | Borrow money, then buy what you want. |
| Rent what you want. | Save money, then rent what you want. |

With the two-stage strategies, you first do one thing and then another. The *order* in which you do these things makes a difference. If you can't afford what you want, saving money and buying is a possible strategy, but buying and then saving doesn't make sense. In general, when a strategy has more than one stage, the order of the stages makes a big difference. That's why planning is important.

A strategy can also have more than two stages. Suppose you want to use the strategy to borrow money and then buy what you want, but no one will lend you the money. You might use a three-stage strategy: become credit-worthy, borrow money, and then buy what you want.

After you choose a strategy, you usually have a lot of choices at each stage. In a save-and-buy strategy, for example, you could save money in different ways. You could get a second job, earn interest on your savings, give up ice cream, walk instead instead of ride, and so on. You could also buy in different ways. You could go to just one store, visit several stores to compare prices and quality, look at advertisements, place your own ad, or whatever. The choices you have for carrying out a particular strategy are called *tactics*. For example, getting a second job and walking instead of riding are tactics for the save-money strategy.

Strategy and tactics are often talked about in connection with war. War itself, for that matter, is just one strategy for a country to reach its goals; negotiation is another. Assume that a country's strategy is to cut off new supplies from reaching its enemy. Its tactics might then be blockade, persuading other countries not to trade with its enemy, interdictory bombing, and other measures.

In our daily lives we sometimes have struggles that seem like mini-wars between child and parent, between husband and wife, between employee and boss, between salesperson and customer, between teacher and student. You can be more successful in these struggles if you are good at developing strategies and tactics. For example:

1. Two parents want their child to help more with household chores. Among their possible strategies are ordering the child to do the chores, setting up a system of cooperatively sharing the chores, and paying the child to do the chores. If they choose the

paying strategy, then they must decide about tactics, such as whether to pay the child a flat amount each week or a certain amount for each chore. If the latter, should they pay as soon as the chore is completed or at the end of the week? And so on.

2. A woman has a dispute with a store owner about some merchandise that turned out to be unsatisfactory. Among her possible strategies are taking the matter to court, urging her friends not to shop in that store, and talking the matter over with the store owner. If she chooses the talk-it-over strategy, she must then decide on tactics: She could demand a refund of her money, request an exchange of merchandise, or return the merchandise for a credit, among other possibilities.

3. A basketball coach may decide that the team should emphasize either offense or defense, both in its practice sessions and in actual games. If the coach chooses offense, she might further choose a "fast-break" pattern as a tactic; if she chooses defense, she might further choose a zone defense as a tactic.

In other situations, even though you don't struggle against someone else, the *ideas* of strategy and tactics are nevertheless important.

1. Two people think the strategy of getting a college degree will help them get better jobs. Both are poor in math. One uses the tactic of avoiding courses that involve math, while the other uses the tactic of getting a tutor in math.

2. Two other people think the strategy of impressing the boss will help them advance in their jobs. One chooses the tactic of working hard, and the other the tactic of looking very busy.

In many life situations, good strategy and good tactics are important. Choosing good strategy and choosing good tactics are skills that, just like serving and backhand strokes in tennis, can be improved through exercise. This chapter gives you opportunities to exercise these skills in many different kinds of games. All the games are aimed at developing your strategic skill, just as you can do many different physical exercises to strengthen a muscle.

Now here's the plan for the rest of the chapter: We present many groups of card games. The first game in each group is the easiest, and we fully explain how to get the most benefit in developing strategy skill from playing it. The other games in the group slowly get harder. You may begin with any game in the first group. If it is too hard, try an earlier one; if it is too easy, try a later one. If the last game in the group is too easy, move to the next group. After the games come everyday situations, to which you can apply the strategy skills you have learned. Throughout the chapter, we discuss general principles of strategy and how to use them.

Ready? Let's get started.

## REMOVING CARDS BY A JUMP-AND-TAKE RULE

Each game in the first group has the same goal: to get rid of all the cards but one. To succeed, you must plan ahead. If you don't plan ahead, you will be left with more than one card.

## SM 1–1 (LL)
### RULES OF THE GAME

*Aim of the Game*: To remove four out of five cards by using a jump-and-take rule.

*Number of Players*: One.

*Materials Needed*: Five cards; grid 4×7.

*Preparation*: The cards are placed face down in the positions shown below. For convenience, we label the cards from 1 to 5.

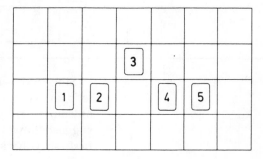

*How to Play:* The player makes a series of moves. On each move, the player picks one card to jump over another, horizontally or vertically, to an empty square just beyond. The card jumped over is then removed. The game continues until only one card remains.

## SM 1–2 (ML)

Following the same rules, player must remove *all but one* card from each starting position.

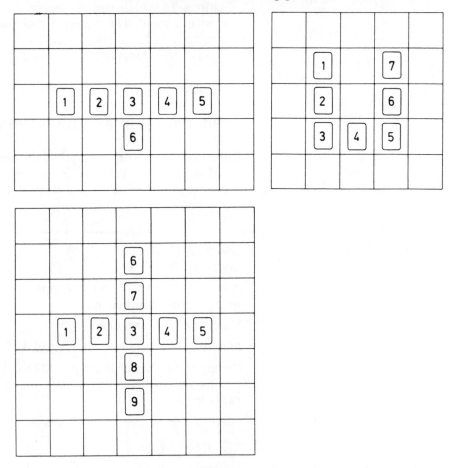

Since SM 1–1 (LL) represents our first strategy game, let's go over the rules very carefully together. You may of course use *any* five cards to play this game. We suggest, however, that you use the ace through 5 at first, so you can follow our analysis better and keep track of your moves.

You must make a series of moves, jumping one card over another and removing the card that was jumped over. You might begin by jumping 2 over 1, and removing 1. Or you could jump the 4 over the 5, removing the 5. Can you see any other possible first moves? Stop reading, and see if you can find *all* the possible first moves. . . . Did you find two more we didn't show you?

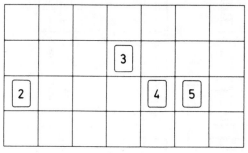

2 over 1

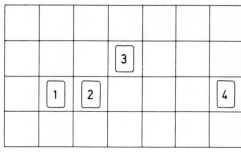

4 over 5

They are jumping the 1 over the 2 and removing the 2, or jumping the 5 over the 4 removing the 4. So you can begin by moving the 1, 2, 4, or 5. But you cannot begin by moving the 3, because it has no card, horizontally or vertically, to jump over. Now that you know all the possible first moves, play a few complete games to get familiar with what works and what doesn't.

If you now, after playing a game or two, have had some wins (you removed four of the five cards) and some losses (more than one card was left when you couldn't move any more), let's analyze the game together. The chart on page 92 shows the different ways the game may turn out. At the top, you see the beginning position of the cards. As you already know, four different moves are possible at the beginning. The chart shows the positions (A, B, C, and D) you would get from each of these four moves, with lines drawn to them from the beginning positions.

But how different are these four "different" positions? C is really the same as D, only flipped over. If you actually fold one half of the book page over the other and peep through, you see that the positions of the cards would be the same in C and D. When two such positions are the same as each other but flipped over like that, we say the two positions are *symmetrical* to each other. In this game, C is symmetrical to D. For

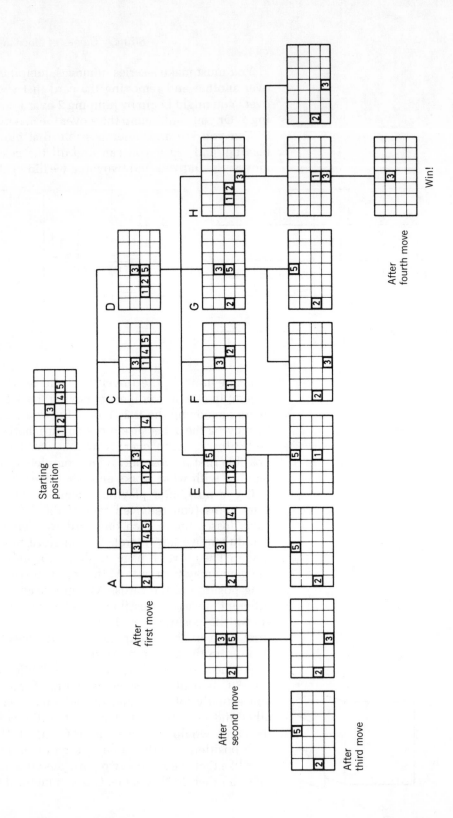

Starting
position

After
first move

After
second move

After
third move

After
fourth move

Win!

A

B

C

D

E

F

G

H

any move you make from C, you could make a symmetrical move from D. Further, the *next* positions in each case will *also* be symmetrical! For example:

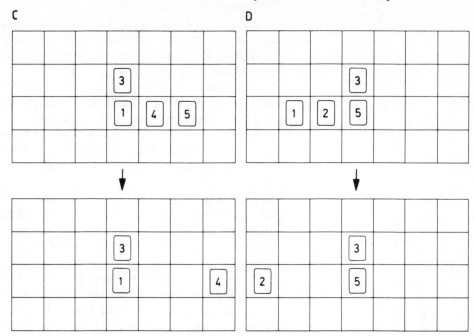

Symmetry is important in this game because it makes our analysis simpler. Have you noticed that A is symmetrical to B? After the first move, we have only two *really* different positions, A and D. In our chart, then, we show you only what could happen next from positions A and D. (You can check that B and C give you symmetrical results.)

To keep things simple, we will say that after our first move we have either position A or D.

Let's try A. From A, we have two possible moves. The 4 can jump over 5, or 5 can jump over 4. The chart shows what happens in each case. If 4 jumps over 5, there is no next move possible, and we lose. If 5 jumps over 4, the chart shows us two more possible moves. The 5 jumps over 3, or 3 jumps over 5. In each case we lose. We see that, if we first move to position A, we must lose.

Let's try D. From here we have *four* possible moves:

- 5 jumps over 3.
- 2 jumps over 1.
- 2 jumps over 5.
- 3 jumps over 5.

In the chart these moves lead to positions E, F, G, and H. Since none of them is symmetrical to another, we must consider all four.

The chart shows that F leads to no more moves; we lose. Each of E, G, and H leads to two possible other moves. But the chart shows that only H may lead to a win: from H, if 1 jumps over 2, we can win on the next move. But if 2 jumps over 1, we lose.

To summarize, at first we have four choices: A, B, C, and D. A is symmetrical to B, and C is symmetrical to D. We can simply consider A and D, ignoring B and C. A always loses. D leads to four choices. Of these choices, E, F, and G always lose. Only H may be a winner.

Since positions A, E, F, and G always lose, let's look below at what they have in common (don't let your inductive logic muscle lose its strength!) In each case, one card has become separated from the others by more than one square. When you let this happen, you lose. By careful planning—you can avoid these situations and win!

You have learned the winning strategy in this game. You have also learned that you can ignore one of two symmetrical positions. This lesson helps you to develop a strategy, because you have fewer possibilities to think about.

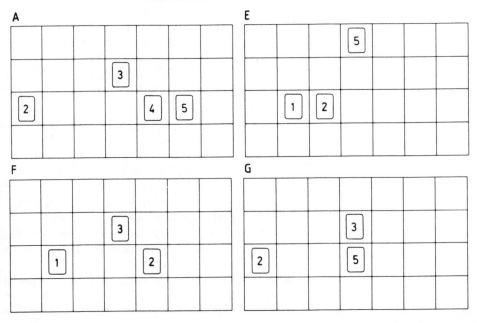

In other games, too, sometimes you can ignore certain possibilities and concentrate on your strategy better. We will point out these occasions as we go along.
As for SM 1–2, the solutions are:

- 6 cards: Jump the 6 over the 3, then continue as in SM 1–1.
- 7 cards: Jump 4, 1, 4, 4, 7, 4.
- 9 cards: Jump 8, 7, 1, 1, 8, 5, 8, 6.

## REMOVING CARDS BY JUMP-AND-TAKE RULE: TWO PLAYERS, 24 CARDS

Each game in the last group was set up so that you could *always* win by jumping if you had the right strategy. In the next group of games, however, the beginning position of the cards is set up by chance, and you may not always be able to take away all the cards but one.

## SM 2–1 (HL)
### RULES OF THE GAME

*Aim of the Game*: To remove all but one of the randomly placed cards by using a jump-and-take rule.

*Number of Players*: Two.

*Materials Needed*: 24 cards from each deck; grid 8×8.

*Preparation*: The top 24 cards from each shuffled deck are placed up, as shown on the next page. Then all the clubs are removed, to make more room for jumping. The remaining cards are turned face down to distinguish the red and blue groups (each player's separate color).

*How to Play*: Player *A* uses the red cards, player *B* the blue. The players alternate turns. On each turn, the player picks one card to jump over another, horizontally or vertically, to an empty square just beyond. The player may continue jumping over other cards on the same turn if the squares beyond are empty. The cards jumped over are then removed. A player without a jump to make loses a turn. The game continues until no more cards can be removed. The player with fewer cards left on the grid is the winner.

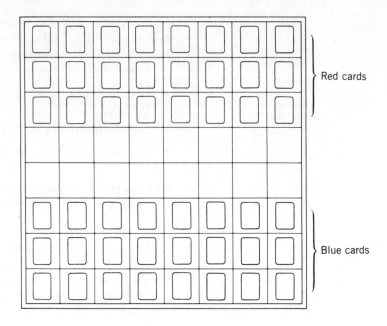

Red cards

Blue cards

## SM 2–2 (HL)

Same as SM 2–1, except 32, instead of 24, cards from each deck are dealt out at first, covering the entire grid.

---

### REMOVING CARDS BY JUMP-AND-TAKE RULE: TWO PLAYERS AND 24 CARDS, WITH MOVES

In the next group of games, the beginning position of the cards is again set up by chance. But the rules allow you to move cards horizontally or vertically to adjacent squares to get into better positions for jumping.

---

## SM 3–1 (HL)

#### RULES OF THE GAME

*Aim of the Game*: To remove all but one of the randomly placed cards by moving them and using a jump-and-take rule.

*Number of Players*: Two.

*Materials Needed*: 24 cards from each deck; grid 8×8.

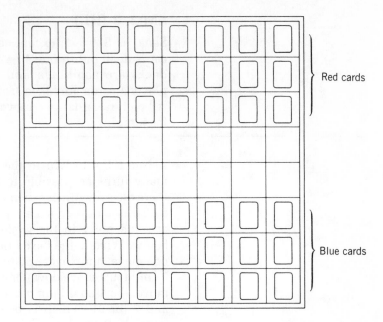

*Preparation*: The top 24 cards from each shuffled deck are placed face up, as shown above. Then all the clubs are removed, to make more room for jumping. The remaining cards are turned face down to distinguish the red and blue groups (each player's separate color).

*How to Play*: Player *A* uses the red cards, player *B* the blue. The players alternate turns. On each turn the player can:

1. move a card horizontally or vertically to an adjacent empty square, or
2. jump one card over another, horizontally or vertically, to an empty square just beyond, and continue jumping over other cards on the same turn if the squares beyond are empty. The cards jumped over are then removed.

The game continues until one player is down to a single card. That player wins.

## SM 3–2 (HL)

Same as SM 3–1, except deal out 32, instead of 24, cards from each deck at first, covering the entire grid.

### SM 3–3 (HL)

Same as SM 3–1, except each of *four* players gets 16 cards dealt out in one 4×4 *corner* of the grid. The two decks are combined and sorted out by suit. Each player's cards are taken from a different shuffled suit. All picture cards are removed so that there will be room for jumping.

---

Naturally, to win in the fewest turns, you want as many turns as possible to be jumps, not moves. Yet there are some times when the best strategy is to use up a turn as a move, not a jump. For example, suppose that at some point in the game the position is as shown below. What is the best strategy now? The 5 could, in one move, jump over and remove the 6, 7, and 3. Or the 5 could just move down one square, so that, on the next move, the 1 could jump over and remove the 4, 5, 6, 2, and 7 (or 3). Which is better? You'll have to see for yourself. Each shuffle gives you a new opportunity to plan your strategy.

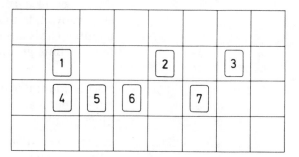

**CHANGING PLACES IN THE SAME ROW**

This group of games also gives you practice planning ahead, but toward a different kind of goal. Instead of trying to *remove* cards from the grid, your goal will be to *move them into particular positions* on the grid.

---

### SM 4–1 (LL)
**RULES OF THE GAME**

*Aim of the Game:* To bring the two blue cards to the left of the two red cards.

Starting position

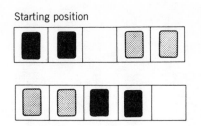

*Number of Players:* One.

*Materials Needed:* Two blue cards, two red cards; grid 1×5.

*Preparation:* Two blue cards and two red cards are placed face down in the positions shown at the left.

*How to Play:* The player takes a series of turns. On each turn, a card can move to the next square if empty, or it can jump over one or two other cards, blue or red, to reach an empty square. The game ends when all the cards are in the goal position.

*Remark:* Practice so that you can do it in fewer moves.

## SM 4–2 (LL)

Following the same rules, the player must bring the three blue cards to the left of the three red cards. The starting positions and goals are as follows:

Starting position

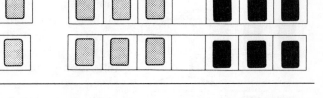

a.

b.

Let's look first at SM 4–1. The kinds of moves allowed are shown at the left. It is a simple game with a simple strategy. Play it a few times. Can you say what the strategy is? Here's how we can state the strategy: On each move, make the choice that gets you closer to your goal.

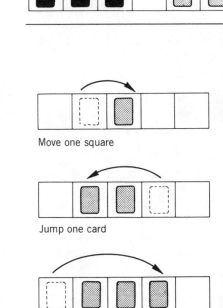

Move one square

Jump one card

Jump two cards

Let's show how this strategy works so that you can apply it to other, more complicated games. Look at the difference between the starting position and the goal. What distance do all the cards together have to move to go from the starting position to the goal? If the red card that starts in square A winds up in C, and the red card that starts in B winds up in D, each goes a distance of two squares, for a total of four squares. Also, if the red card that starts in square A winds up in D, and the red card that starts in B winds up in C, they move three and one squares, for a total of four squares. Either way, then, the red cards must go a distance of four squares.

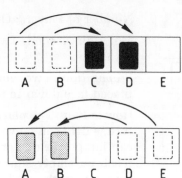

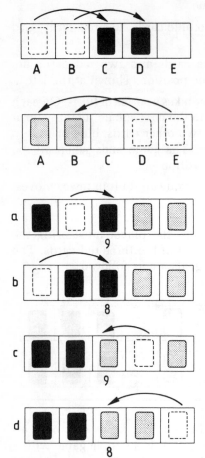

No matter which blue card winds up in A and which in B, the blue cards must go a distance of six squares. All the cards together, then, must move a total distance of ten squares.

If our strategy is to, on each move, make the choice that gets you closer to your goal, this means that, on each move, *reduce by as much as possible* the total distance that the cards must move. So if at the start the total distance is ten squares, a move that reduces this to eight is better than a move that reduces it only to nine.

Let's see how this strategy applies to the choice of the first move. The possible moves are shown to the left, along with the total distance remaining if that move were taken. (b) and (d) are the better moves. How could we choose between them? Look at what the best moves would be after (b) and (d). Here they are:

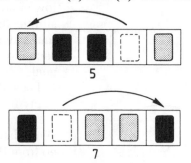

The move that follows (b) would bring us closer to the goal. In fact, just two more moves would be needed:

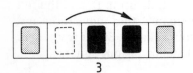

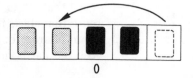

Let's summarize the strategy for this game in a general way, so you can apply it to other games:

1. Find a way to measure the difference between the starting position and the goal.
2. On each move, make the choice that reduces this distance the most.

Naturally, this strategy does not apply to all games. For some games, you may not be able to measure the distance between the starting situation and the goal. In other games, you may be able to measure it, but it's not always the best strategy to reduce it as much as possible on each move. Sometimes it may be better to choose either a move that reduces the distance less than another does or one that actually *increases* it.

Why, then, should you bother to know this strategy? The reason is that it is useful to have in your kit of "strategy tools" when you play a game for the first time. You should try it out, but not follow it blindly.

## CHANGING PLACES IN THE GRID

In the last group of games, your aim was to put cards into particular positions on the grid, but the rules didn't tell you which specific cards to put into which positions. The games in this group require you to put specific cards into particular positions.

## SM 5–1 (LL)

### RULES OF THE GAME

Starting position

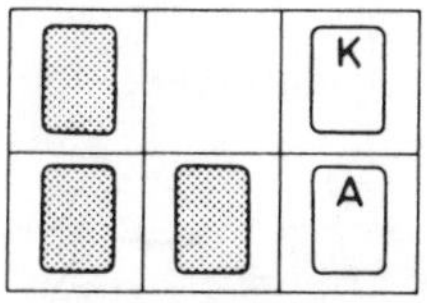

Goal

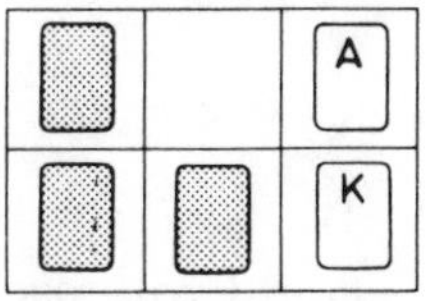

*Aim of the Game*: To change the places of the king and ace by moving cards one square at a time, horizontally or vertically only.

*Number of Players*: One.

*Materials Needed*: King, ace, three face-down cards; grid 2×3.

*Preparation*: A king and ace are placed face up, along with three face-down cards in the positions shown to the left.

*How to Play*: The player makes a series of moves. On each move one card may be shifted horizontally or vertically to an adjacent empty square. No diagonal moves are allowed. The game ends when the king and ace have changed places with each other. Fewer moves are better.

### SM 5–2 (LL)

The same rules as SM 5–1, but the starting position and goal are as follows:

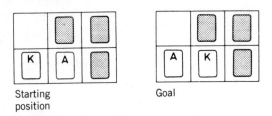

Starting position          Goal

---

Play this game a while to get familiar with it. . . . Have you found a winning strategy? One way to build a winning strategy is to work backwards. Ask yourself, "From which position could I win easily?" That position is called a *subgoal*. Then ask, "From which position could I reach the subgoal?" That position is an earlier subgoal. Keep finding earlier and earlier subgoals until you are at the starting position. Then go forward, reaching each subgoal in turn, until you reach the goal.

Let's see just how this idea works. Suppose the cards were in this position:

$$
\begin{array}{ccc}
X & X & - \\
X & K & 1
\end{array}
$$

You could win easily in two moves:

$$
\begin{array}{ccc}
X & X & - \\
X & K & 1
\end{array}
\longrightarrow
\begin{array}{ccc}
X & X & 1 \\
X & K & -
\end{array}
\longrightarrow
\begin{array}{ccc}
X & X & 1 \\
X & - & K
\end{array}
$$

So,

$$
\begin{array}{ccc}
X & X & - \\
X & K & 1
\end{array}
$$

is your last subgoal. How could you reach it?

First, let's see what is important about this position. If the empty square were in a different position, such as:

$$\begin{matrix} X & X & X \\ - & K & 1 \end{matrix} \longrightarrow \begin{matrix} - & X & X \\ X & K & 1 \end{matrix} \longrightarrow \begin{matrix} X & - & X \\ X & K & 1 \end{matrix} \longrightarrow \begin{matrix} X & X & - \\ X & K & 1 \end{matrix}$$

you could easily get to the subgoal. The position of the empty square is not important. The important thing about the last subgoal is that the king and the ace are next to each other on the bottom row, with the king on the left.

Suppose the king and the ace were both on the bottom row, with the king on the left, but there was a card in between them:

$$\begin{matrix} X & - & X \\ K & X & 1 \end{matrix}$$

Could you reach the last subgoal from this position? Of course. First move:

$$\begin{matrix} X & - & X \\ K & X & 1 \end{matrix} \longrightarrow \begin{matrix} X & X & X \\ K & - & 1 \end{matrix} \longrightarrow \begin{matrix} X & X & X \\ - & K & 1 \end{matrix}$$

Then move the empty square around.

So the next-to-last subgoal is to have the king, another card, and then the ace from left to right on the bottom row. How could you reach this next-to-last subgoal? Suppose the cards were in this position:

$$\begin{matrix} X & X & 1 \\ 1 & K & X \end{matrix}$$

Now the king, another card, then the ace are almost in left-to-right order in the bottom row, but the "bottom row" goes around a corner!

$$\begin{matrix} & 1 & \\ K & X & \end{matrix}$$

You could shift these three important cards, one at a time, to get them into the bottom row position you want.

So X, X, 1 is the subgoal before the next-to-last sub-goal –, K, X. How could you reach it? If the cards were in the position

```
X  K  1

X  –  X
```

you could just shift the king down to reach the subgoal. The important thing about

```
X  K  1
X  –  X
```

is that the king and ace are next to each other on the top row, with the king on the left. And this is very close to our starting position. Can you see how to go from

```
X  –  K   to   X  K  1
X  X  1        X  –  X ?
```

We have worked backwards from the goal to the starting positions, picking out subgoals along the way. Now let's summarize in the forwards direction. Following are the diagrams for the starting position, each sub-goal, and the final goal. In between the diagrams you are told which moves to make:

```
X  –  K    X  K  1    X  X  1    X  –  X
X  X  1    X  –  X    –  K  X    K  X  1

King left  King down  King left  Card up
Ace up     Card right Card left  King right
Card right Card up    Ace down   Card down
                      Card right Card left
                                 Card left
```

```
X  X  –    X  X  1
X  K  1    X  –  K
Ace up
King right
```

In many games you can build a winning strategy by working backward, as we did here. First you choose a final subgoal, from which you can win easily. Then you pick another subgoal, from which you can reach the first subgoal. Continue in this way until you reach the starting position. Then you go forward, reaching each subgoal in turn and finally reaching the goal.

## MOVING CARDS INTO NUMERICAL ORDER

The next few games give you more practice with setting and reaching subgoals. In each game, you must move *every* card into a particular position.

### SM 6–1 (ML)
**RULES OF THE GAME**

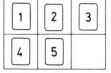

Starting
position

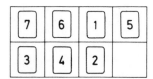

Goal

*Aim of the Game*: To get five cards in numerical order by moving them horizontally and vertically.

*Number of Players*: One.

Materials Needed: Ace through five; grid 2×3.

*Preparation*: Cards are placed face up in the starting position shown at the left.

*How to Play*: The player makes a series of moves. On each move, a card may be shifted horizontally or vertically to an adjacent empty square. Game ends when the goal position is reached. Fewer moves are better.

### SM 6–2 (ML)
Same rules as SM 6–1, with 1–7 used in a 2×4 grid, instead of 1–5 in a 2×3 grid. The starting position and goal are as shown.

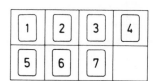

Goal

### SM 6–3 (HL)
Same rules as SM 6–1, with 1–jack used in a 3×4 grid, instead of 1–5 in a 2–3 grid. The starting position and goal are as shown.

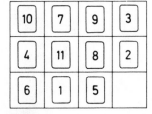

Starting
position

Goal

### SM 6–4 (HL)

Same rules and goals as SM 6–1, 6–2, or 6–3, but with the starting position chosen at random by shuffling and dealing out cards, instead of a fixed starting position.

*Warning:* It may not always be possible to reach the goal from all starting positions.

Try game SM 6–1. Can you reach the goal? Now see the *fewest* number of moves in which you can reach the goal. . . . Have you done it in ten moves? Here's how you can: First move card 2, then 3, 1, 2, 3, 5, 4, 1, 2, 3.

### SM 7–1 (HL)
#### RULES OF THE GAME

*Aim of the Game:* To get all fourteen randomly placed cards into numerical order, beginning with *any* card in the upper left, by moving them horizontally and vertically.

*Number of Players:* Two.

*Materials Needed:* Deck of cards; grey cards to mark off borders; grid 2×3.

Starting position

| 4 | 5 | 6 | 7 | 8 | | | |
|---|---|---|---|---|---|---|---|
| 9 | 10 | 11 | 12 | 13 | | | |
| 14 | 1 | 2 | 3 | | | | |
| | | | | | | | |
| | | | | | | | |
| | | 8 | 9 | 10 | 11 | 12 | |
| | | 13 | 14 | 1 | 2 | 3 | |
| | | 4 | 5 | 6 | 7 | | |

Possible goal positions

*Preparation:* For each player, an ace through king of one suit and a joker are shuffled together and then dealt out face up in one 3×5 corner of the grid as shown:

*How to Play:* The ranks of the cards form an endless chain, with the joker having rank 14. For example: 5, 6, 7, 8, 9, 10, jack, queen, king, joker, 1, 2, 3, 4, 5, 6...

The players alternate moves. On each move a card may be shifted horizontally or vertically to an adjacent empty square within the player's own 3×5 section of the total grid. The first player to get cards in numerical order, beginning with any card in the upper left, wins.

*Warning:* It will not always be possible to reach *any* goal from all starting positions. On each deal you'll have to decide which arrangement of the cards you should try for, and you may have to change your goal.

You can, of course, play this game by yourself by shuffling and dealing out a group of fourteen cards in one corner, and trying to get them into numerical order in as few moves as possible.

### SM 8–1 (LL)
**RULES OF THE GAME**

*Aim of the Game*: To get your four cards to the opposite corner by moves or by jumps-without-taking in four turns.

*Number of Players*: One.

*Materials Needed*: Four red cards; grid 4×4.

*Preparation*: The four cards are placed face down in the starting position shown at the left.

*How to play*: The player takes a series of turns. On each turn either a card is moved horizontally, vertically or diagonally to an adjacent empty square, or it jumps over an adjacent card to an empty square just beyond it. A card may make more than one jump in succession on the same turn. The cards jumped over are *not* removed. The game continues until all four cards are in the opposite corner from where they began, in the squares marked by Xs.

### SM 8–2 (ML)
Same as SM 8–1, but with a 5×5 grid, instead of 4×4 (case A), or with a 5×5 grid, instead of 4×4, and 10 cards instead of 4 (case B).

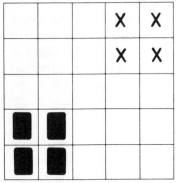

Case A

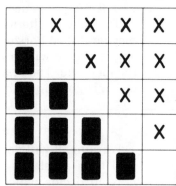

Case B

In this simple game, (SM 8–1), you can begin 16 different ways! Some are *moves*, shown by a *solid*

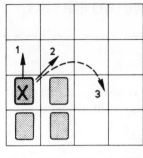

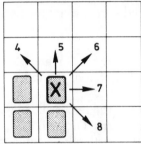

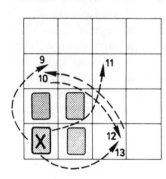

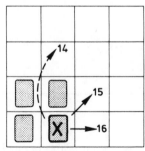

arrow (———►), and some are *jumps*, shown by a dashed arrow (— — —►). All 16 are shown at the left. But you want to get the four cards into the opposite corner in just *four* moves. This means you must get one card into the opposite corner on each move. You can therefore eliminate 14 of the 16 moves that don't do this for you. You are left with two possibilities:

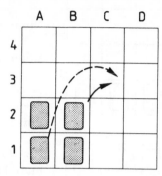

If you move B2–C3, there's no way to get a second card into the opposite corner on the second move. So your first move must be:

1. A1 to C3.

It can be followed by:

2. A2 to C2 to C4.
3. B1 to B3 to D3.
4. B2 to D4.

Here's how to win at SM 8–2A and SM 8–2B:

| | *2A* | *2B* |
|---|---|---|
| 1. | A1 to C3 | D1 to E2 |
| 2. | A2 to C2 to C4 | A4 to B5 |
| 3. | B1 to B3 to D5 | B1 to D3 |
| 4. | B2 to D4 | B2 to D2 to D4 |
| 5. | C3 to C5 to E5 | A3 to C3 to E3 |
| 6. | C4 to E4 | A1 to A3 to C3 to E5 |
| 7. | | A2 to C4 |
| 8. | | C1 to C3 to C5 |
| 9. | | B3 to D5 |
| 10. | | C2 to E4 |

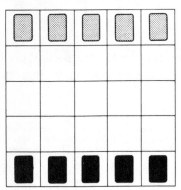

Starting position

Goal

## SM 9–1 (LL)
**RULES OF THE GAME**

*Aim of the Game*: To get your cards to the opposite row by moves and by jumping-without-taking.

*Number of Players*: Two.

*Materials Needed*: Five red cards, five blue cards; grid 5×5.

*Preparation*: Cards of the same color are placed face down in opposite rows as shown at the left.

*How to Play*: Player A moves the red cards, player B the blue. The players alternate turns. On each turn, either a card is moved horizontally, vertically, or diagonally to an adjacent empty square, or it jumps over an adjacent card to an empty square just beyond it. A card may make more than one jump in succession on the same turn. A card may jump over another card of *either* player. Cards that are jumped over are *not* removed.

The first to get all of his or her cards in the row from which the other player's cards began is the winner.

## MOVING CORNER TO CORNER: ONE TO FOUR PLAYERS

### SM 10–1 (ML)
**RULES OF THE GAME**

*Aim of the Game*: To be first to get your six cards to the opposite corner by moves or by jumping-without-taking in four turns.

*Number of Players*: Two to four.

*Materials Needed*: Six cards of each suit; grid 6×6.

Preparation: Each player has six cards of the same suit placed face up in one corner of the grid as shown at the left.

When two play, red and blue cards may be used face down instead of two different suits face up. Each player's cards should start in opposite corners.

When three play, they should take turns in successive games having no cards in the opposite corner.

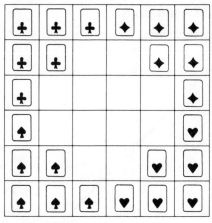

Starting position
for 4 (SM 10–1)

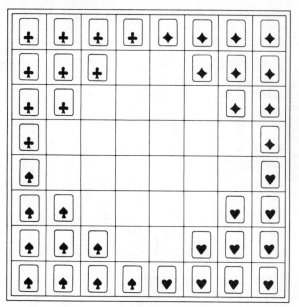

Starting position
for 4 (SM 10–2)

*How to Play*: The players alternate turns. On each turn, either a card is moved horizontally, vertically, or diagonally to an adjacent empty square, or it jumps over an adjacent card to an empty square just beyond it. A card may make more than one jump in succession on the same turn. A card may jump over another card of *any* player. Cards that are jumped over are *not* removed.

The first to get all of his or her cards in the opposite corner is the winner.

*Remark*: This game can also be played by just one player. The object is then to get the cards to the opposite corner in the fewest moves possible.

## SM 10–2 (HL)

Same as SM 10–1, but with ten cards for each player on an 8×8 grid, as shown, instead of six cards on a 6×6 grid.

The strategy in this game is to build up chains of cards so that you can make many multiple jumps, without letting the other players do the same. Here are four basic multiple-jump situations.

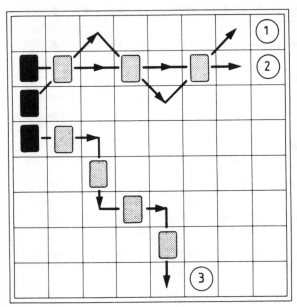

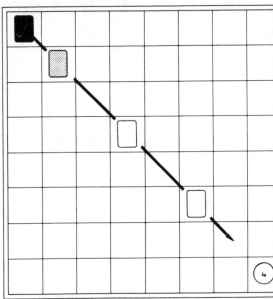

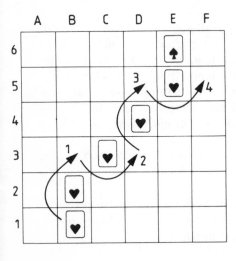

In the situation to the left, the hearts player has set up a chain in which one card can go from B1 to B3, D3, D5, and F5—all in one move. But the spades player can use the same chain to go from E6, to E4, C4, C2, and A2 all in the same move.

### OBTAINING CARDS WITH SEQUENCE

In this game, you again have to get your cards to the opposite corner by moves and jumps. But each card must go into a particular location in the opposite corner.

## SM 11–1 (HL)
### RULES OF THE GAME

*Aim of the Game:* To be first to get each of your cards into specific locations in the opposite row by moves or by jumping-without-taking.

*Number of Players:* Two.

*Materials Needed:* Aces through 6s (1–6) of hearts and of spades; grid 6×8.

*Preparation:* Each player has six cards of the same suit placed face up in opposite rows of the grid as shown.

Starting position

Goal

*How to Play:* The players alternate turns. On each turn, either a card is moved horizontally, vertically or diagonally to an adjacent empty square, or it jumps over an adjacent card to an empty square just beyond it. A card may make more than one jump in succession on the same turn. A card may jump over another card of *either* player. Cards that are jumped over are *not* removed.

The first to get all of his or her cards into the opposite row, in the specific locations shown, wins.

## SM 11–2 (HL)

Same as SM 11–1, except the cards begin and end in specific locations in opposite *corners*, instead of rows, as shown.

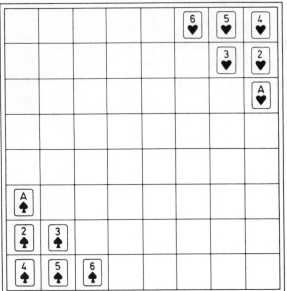

Starting position

Goal

## SM 11–3 (HL)

Same as SM 11–2, but with *four* players instead of two, with each starting in a corner.

*Remark:* These games can also be played by just one player. The object is then to get the cards to the specific locations in the opposite *corner* or *row* in the fewest moves possible.

## CHANGING COLUMNS

## SM 12–1 (LL)
### RULES OF THE GAME

*Aim of the Game:* To get three cards that start in a particular order in one column, into the same order in another column, by moving them one at a time.

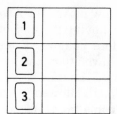

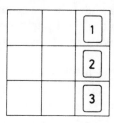

Starting position

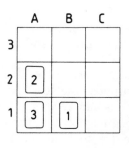

Goal

*Number of Players*: One.

*Materials Needed*: The 1, 2, and 3 (1–3) of one suit; grid 3×3.

*Preparation*: A 1, 2, and 3 are placed face up in that order from top to bottom in the left column of the grid as shown at the left.

*How to Play*: The player moves one card at a time to another column. Player can move any card that is by itself in a column. If there are two or more cards in a column, player can move only the top card. A card cannot be placed into a column that already has cards of a lower rank in it. *A card can be placed only in the lowest empty square of another column.* The 3 has the highest rank, the 1 the lowest.

### SM 12–2 (ML)
Same as SM 12–1, but using 1–4, in a 4×3 grid, instead of 1–3 in a 3×3 grid.

### SM 12–3 (HL)
Same as SM 12–1, but using 1–5, in a 5×3 grid, instead of 1–3 in a 3×3 grid.

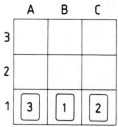

Let's begin with SM 12–1 and look at what the rules allow us to do in this game. At the start, we can move only the ace, because that is the only card at the top of a column. Where can we place the ace? A card is always moved to another column. It's now in column A, so we could move it to Column B or C. We can only place it in B1 or C1, since those are the lowest empty squares of the other columns.

Let's say we place it in B1. What can we do next? Now we can move either the ace or the 2, because each is at the head of a column. We could move the ace to A3, back to where it started from, or to C1, where we could have moved it in the first place. Those possible moves don't interest us so much.

Let's see what we can do with the 2. Since the 2 is now in column A, we can consider moving it to columns B and C. We can't put it in column B, because a card of lower rank, the ace, is already in that column. So we must put the 2 into column C. It goes into C1, the lowest empty square.

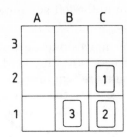

What moves can we now make? We haven't touched the 3 yet. Let's consider moving it out of column A and into column B or C. Both columns B and C already contain cards of rank lower than the 3, so we can't move the 3.

How about the 2? We are allowed to move it to A2, but that's where it just came from. We are *not* allowed to move it to B2. (Do you know why?) We could move the ace either to A2 or C2. Let's try C2. We now have two of the cards, the ace and 2, in the column we want them to be in, but not in the right positions within that column. And finally we are allowed to move the 3—into B1.

Now you're familiar with what the rules allow and what they don't. Place the cards back in their starting positions and see if you can find the winning strategy for this game before you read further. . . .

This is another game that makes subgoals pay off. Suppose you knew how to get both the ace and the 2 from one column into another. You could put them into B and the 3 into C. Since you know how to get the ace and the 2 into another column, you could then use your know-how to get them from B to C! Your strategy has four stages:

1. Learn how to get the ace and 2 from one column to another.

2. Put the ace and 2 into column B.

3. Put the 3 into column C.

4. Put the ace and 2 into column C and win!

Stage 1 is the key: Learn how to put the ace and 2 into another column. Suppose the ace, 2, and 3 are all in column A. What tactics can you use to get the ace and 2 into B? You can begin by putting the 1 into either B or C. If you put the 1 into B, it blocks you from putting the 2 into B. But if you put the 1 into C, you can put the 2 into B, and then put the 1 into B above it. The complete set of moves to win is shown on page 117.

Practice this strategy until you know it thoroughly.

You can directly apply what you learned in SM 12–1 to develop a strategy to win in SM 12–2. Do you see how? Think about it before you read further. . . .

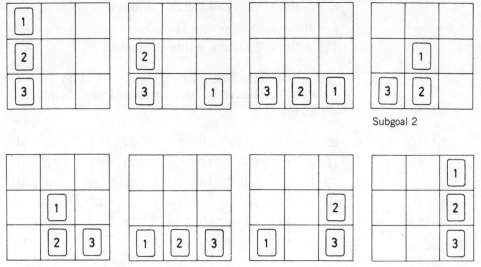

Subgoal 2

Subgoal 3

You already know from SM 12–1 how to get the 1, 2, and 3 from one column to another. Here, then, is the simple three-stage strategy for the present game:

1. Put the 1, 2, and 3 into column B
2. Put the 4 into column C.
3. Put the 1, 2, and 3 into column C.

Can you follow this strategy and win? Play several games so you know the strategy thoroughly. If you need help, here's the complete set of moves, where "1B" means move the ace to column B, and so on.

| 1. | 1B | 6. | 2B | 11. | 1A |
|----|----|----|----|-----|----|
| 2. | 2C | 7. | 1B | 12. | 3C |
| 3. | 1C | 8. | 4C | 13. | 1B |
| 4. | 3B | 9. | 1C | 14. | 2C |
| 5. | 1A | 10. | 2A | 15. | 1C |

Now you can directly apply what you learned in SM 12–2 to develop a strategy to win in SM 12–3. Do you see how? Think about it before you read further. . . .

You already know from SM 12–2 how to get the 1, 2, 3, and 4 from one column to another. Here, then, is the simple three-stage strategy for SM 12–3:

1. Put the 1, 2, 3, and 4 into column B.
2. Put the 5 into column C.
3. Put the 1, 2, 3, and 4 into column C.

Can you follow this strategy and win? Play several games so you know the strategy thoroughly. If you need help, here it is:

| | | | | | | | | | | | |
|---|---|---|---|---|---|---|---|---|---|---|---|
| 1. | 1C | 6. | 2C | 11. | 1A | 16. | 5C | 21. | 1B | 26. | 2B |
| 2. | 2B | 7. | 1C | 12. | 3B | 17. | 1A | 22. | 2A | 27. | 1B |
| 3. | 1B | 8. | 4B | 13. | 1C | 18. | 2C | 23. | 1A | 28. | 3C |
| 4. | 3C | 9. | 1B | 14. | 2B | 19. | 1C | 24. | 4C | 29. | 1A |
| 5. | 1A | 10. | 2A | 15. | 1B | 20. | 3A | 25. | 1C | 30. | 2C |
| | | | | | | | | | | 31. | 1C |

## CHANGING COLUMNS WITH TWO PLAYERS

In the next game, two players compete to be first to move cards, one at a time, from several columns into a particular order in one column.

## SM 13–1 (HL)
### RULES OF THE GAME

*Aim of the Game*: To be first to move cards one at a time from several columns into a particular order in one column.

*Number of Players*: Two.

*Materials Needed*: Aces through the 5s (1–5) of hearts and of spades; grid 5×8.

*Preparation*: Player *A* arranges the hearts face up, one to a square, placing either one or two cards in each column A, B, and C. A higher-ranking card may not be placed above a lower-ranking card in the same column. Player *B* does the same for the spades in columns F, G, and H. Grey cards are placed into columns D and E.

*How to Play*: The players alternate moving one card at a time. Player *B* moves the hearts in columns A, B, and C, while player *A* moves the spades in columns F, G, and H. A player moves one card at a time to another col-

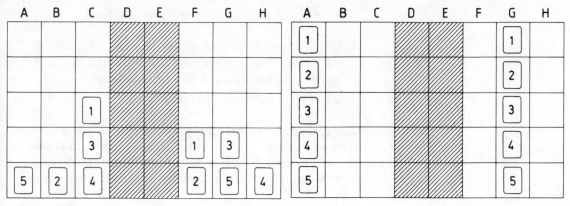

Starting position                                    Goal

umn. A player can move any card that is by itself in a column. If two or more cards are in a column, the player can move only the top card. A card cannot be placed into a column that already has cards of a lower rank in it. A card can be placed only in the lowest empty square of another column. The five has the highest rank, the ace the lowest.

The first player to get all his or her cards into any one column wins.

In this example, a possible strategy for player $B$ is:

1. get the 1 into B,
2. get the 1 and 2 into C, and then
3. get the 1, 2, 3, and 4 into A.

This strategy would take a minimum of 18 moves.
    A possible strategy for player $A$ is:

1. get the 1 and 2 into G,
2. get the 1, 2, and 3 into H, and
3. get 1, 2, 3, and 4 into G.

This strategy would take a minimum of 25 moves. So if each player followed these strategies and played well, player B would win.

    Play this game several times. See if you can develop a general strategy that works *no matter what* the starting position is. . . .

Now see if you can answer these questions:

1. Is it always best to first get the ace and 2 together in the same column, then ace, 2, and 3, then ace, 2, 3, and 4, and finally the ace, 2, 3, 4, and 5?
2. Is it ever a good idea to move the 5?

The answer to the first question is "No." If you began with ace, 2, and 3 in column A, the 5 in column B and the 4 in column C, it would be faster to get the 4 and 5 together in B first. The answer to the second question is "no."

## CREATING ROWS BY PLACING AND MOVING

### SM 14–1 (LL)

**RULES OF THE GAME**

*Aim of the Game*: To be first to get three cards in a row horizontally, vertically, or diagonally by placing or moving them.

*Number of Players*: Two.

*Materials Needed*: Three red and three blue cards; grid 3×3.

*Preparation*: Player *A* is given three red cards, player *B* three blue cards.

*How to Play*: Players alternate turns.

In the first phase, on each turn a player places one card face down on an empty square of the grid. Exception: The first player is not allowed to place a card on the center square (B2) on the first turn.

If there is no winner when all six cards are placed, the game enters the second phase. Players continue to alternate turns; on each turn, a player moves one card horizontally, vertically, or diagonally to an empty adjacent square.

The game ends when one player gets three cards in a row, or when both players agree to a draw.

Starting position

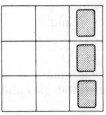

Example of winning position

Here is a play-by-play example of a game between two players, "Red" and "Blue." (See plays 1–4.) On the fourth move, Blue threatens to win at B1, so Red plays there. This defensive move by Red not only saves the game, but it also introduces a threat at A1. Blue stops the threat at A1 and now threatens to win at C3! All the cards are on the grid now. (See plays 5–6.)

The second phase begins, in which cards are moved to adjacent squares. Red cannot get to C3 in time to stop the threat, and Blue wins! (See plays 7–8.)

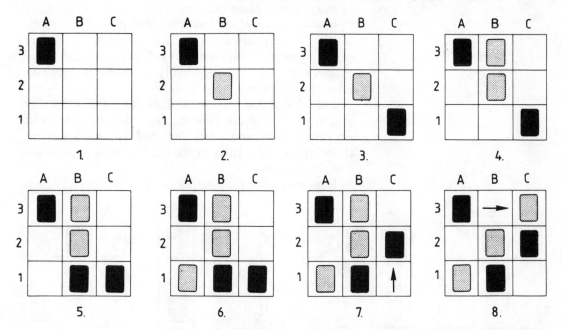

Notice the difference in strategy between this game and ordinary Tic-Tac-Toe. The same first three plays in Tic-Tac-Toe would lead to a game in which Blue would be on the defensive and have to play well just to draw. Yet in this game, after three plays, if Blue knows how to handle the situation, Red has already lost!

What have you learned from this sample game? First of all, you know now how to force a win if you are the second player and the game has begun as shown to the left. It doesn't matter if a red card is first put down in A3 and later in C1, or vice versa. Either way, you can force a win from that beginning position.

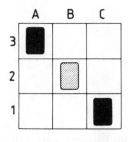

Still, this is a very specific thing to learn. How can we make it more general? You can also force a win if

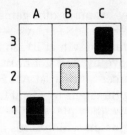

the game begins as shown at the left, because this beginning position is symmetrical to the other. (See page
91 if you've forgotten what this means.) And it doesn't
matter if a red card were put down first in A1 and later
in C3, or vice versa.

Either of the two beginning positions, then, is a subgoal for you, if you are the second player. And each is a
position you should avoid if you are the first player.

As the first player, if you begin by putting a card into
a corner, and if your opponent places a card in the
center, do *not* place your next card in the diagonally
opposite corner. If the first player (not you) begins by
putting a card into a corner, you might set a trap by
putting your card into the center. If your opponent next
places a card in the diagonally opposite corner, you
know how to win.

But what if your opponent doesn't continue the way
you want? What are your chances then? Could your
opponent be setting a trap for *you*? You can't answer
these questions until you have a lot more experience
with this game.

Here's another play-by-play example:

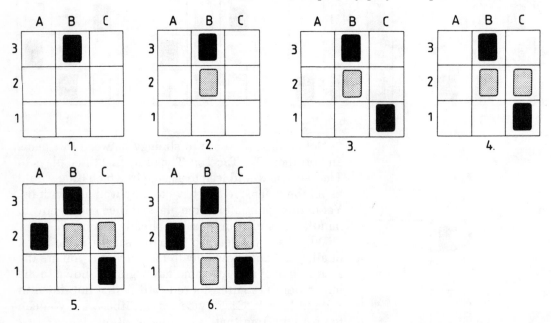

On the fourth move, Blue threatens to win at A2. Red
responds to the threat. (See plays 5–6.) Blue places the

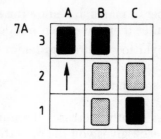

7A

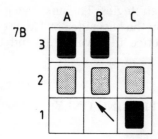

7B

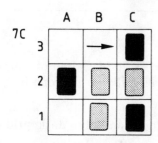

7C

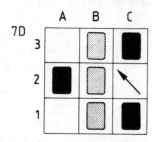

7D

last card on the grid. It is Red's turn to move now, and there does not seem to be a threat. But what can Red do? Should Red move the card at A2, B3, or C1? If a red card is moved out of A2, then Blue wins as shown in plays 7a and 7b. If a red card is moved out of B3, then Blue wins as shown in plays 7c and 7d. And the red card at C1 is blocked from moving at all. Whatever Red does, Blue must win.

From these two sample games of SM 14–1, you can learn some more general strategic principles. They apply to other games too and, as we shall see, to life situations as well:

- A defensive move that stops a threat can also produce a direct threat to win.
- It's possible to win from a position in which you don't make a direct threat.
- "Different" patterns may actually be the same (through symmetry).
- Plan ahead.
- Set up subgoals.
- Watch your opponent's moves.
- Anticipate your opponent's moves.
- Record your moves so you can learn from your experiences.
- Recognize patterns; know what to do with a pattern you recognize.

SM 14–1 is a variation of the well-known game Tic-Tac-Toe, which is itself quickly learned and played. Two players alternately place their own marks on a 3×3 grid. The goal is for a player to place three marks in a row horizontally, vertically, or diagonally. But the possibilities in this game are quite limited, and most people find that, after a little practice, all the games end in a draw. Happily, however, the basic idea of Tic-Tac-Toe can be incorporated into more interesting games in a number of ways:

- by expanding the playing field to 8×8.
- by requiring four or five in a row instead of three,
- by permitting more than two players at a time,

- by limiting the number of marks, but allowing them to move in the grid after they have been put down,
- by allowing each player to capture and remove the other players' marks, or
- by allowing a "row" to bend.

Each of these changes greatly increases the number of possible moves, and each gives you the opportunity to learn and to use new strategies. The next five games, all in some way, build on the basic idea of Tic-Tac-Toe, giving you further practice in developing and using strategies.

### CREATING ROWS BY PLACING ONLY: FOUR IN A ROW

---

### SM 15–1 (ML)
**RULES OF THE GAME**

*Aim of the Game:* To be first to place four of your cards in a row horizontally, vertically, or diagonally.

*Number of Players:* Two.

*Materials Needed:* Red deck and blue deck; grid 8×8.

*How to Play:* Player A uses the red deck, player B the blue deck. Players alternate turns. On each turn a player places one card face down in an empty square on the grid. The game ends when one player gets four cards in a row, or when all the squares on the grid are filled.

---

Here's an example in which Blue went first. The numbers beside the cards show the order in which they were placed down.

1. D4  Blue begins by placing a card into a central position that allows a possible four in a row in eight different directions.

2. F4  Red responds by placing a card near the center. This card cramps Blue's expansion to the right along row 4, but at the same time it limits Red's expansion to the left along row 4.

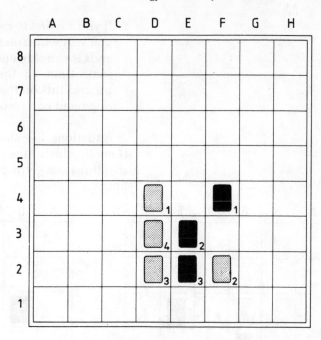

3. F2  Blue threatens to make a diagonal row.

4. E3  Red breaks up Blue's threat, creating Red's own threat of a diagonal row.

5. D2  Blue counters Red's threat, at the same time creating two new threats: a vertical row on column D and a horizontal row in row 2.

At this point, the game is really lost for Red. Red can counter one threat, but not both, in one move. Red plays a card at E2. Blue plays at D3, producing three in a row. Red can now seal off one end, but not both, in one move. Red plays at D5, and Blue plays at D1 to win.

Red could have played at G5, threatening to play at H6 next. But this would not have been an effective threat. Blue could play at H6 first, or ignore the threat.

What strategic principles can you learn from playing this game?

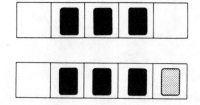

1. Getting three in a row is a subgoal: Your opponent can close only one of those ends on the next move. Of course, the three in a row must be "open" at both ends and not closed at one end, as shown at the left.

2. If you are first to get three in a row open at both ends, you will win. You can get three in a row open at both ends if you threaten in two different directions at the same time. In the preceding game, Blue accomplished this on the fifth move by playing at D2. The opponent can respond to only one of these threats.

Situations 1–4 show some examples of game situations in which Blue plays next. Can you find the move that threatens getting three in a row in *two* directions at once?

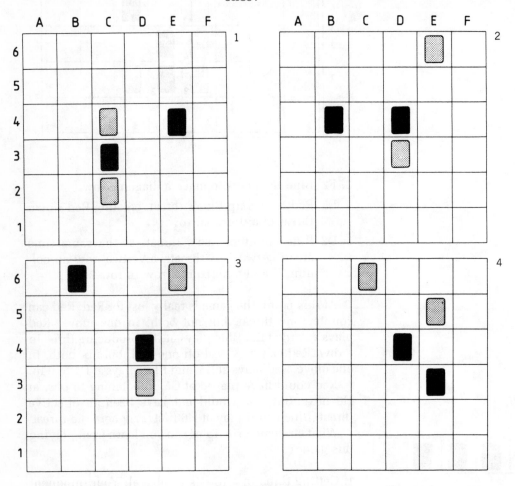

1. B3 or A2 or A4.

2. C4 or E4.

3. C4 or E4. But more important to play C5 to counter Red's threat.

4. C5, D5, D6, or E6. But C5 best, to counter Red's threat at the same time.

You can also learn some more general strategic principles from this game and then apply them to other games, as well to real life situations:

- Set up subgoals
- Work backwards from the goal.
- Watch your opponent's moves.
- Anticipate your opponent's moves.

## CREATING ROWS BY PLACING ONLY: FIVE IN A ROW

In this game, you must get *five* cards in a row.

---

### SM 16–1 (HL)
#### RULES OF THE GAME

*Aim of the Game*: To be first to place five of your cards in a row horizontally, vertically, or diagonally.

*Number of Players*: Two,

*Materials Needed*: Red deck and blue deck; grid 8×8.

*How to Play*: Player A uses the red deck, player B the blue deck. Players alternate turns. On each turn, a player places one card face down in an empty square on the grid. Exception: A card may not be placed where it would set up two rows of exactly three, each open at both ends. Game ends when one player gets five cards in a row or when all the squares on the grid are filled.

---

Before we begin to play and analyze this game, let's first make sure you understand the "exception" in the rules. Look at the situation from the middle of a game shown on p. 128. It is Blue's turn to play. Placing a card at E7 is not allowed, because it would set up two row of exactly three (at E5, E6, E7, and C7, D7, E7), open at all four ends (E4, E8, B7, and F7). But Blue could place a card at B7, setting up a row of *four* and a row of *three*, open at all four ends. The rules permit doing so. This would force a win on Blue's next turn. On the other hand, if Blue does not place a card at B7 or B3, Red can force a win by playing a card at D3 or F4.

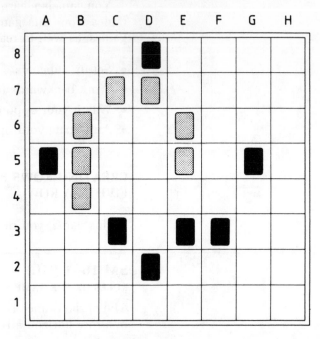

Now that you understand the exception in the rules, play a few games. See what strategic principles you can find for playing this game before you read further. . . .

A subgoal that *must* lead to a win for you (unless your opponent has a good threat going) is to *get a row of four open at both ends*. Of course, your opponent will try to prevent you from doing so. An alert opponent will block you any time you get just three in a row. So, until your opponent catches on, your subgoal could be to place a card that give you two rows of four, each with a gap in it. For example, look at the situation at the left. The four cards seem to be only very loosely connected. But if you place a card at D3, you are suddenly threatening to get four in a row in two different places (by playing next at C3 or E4). If your opponent has no threat going, you will win.

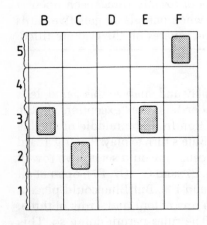

In each of the following situations, it is your turn as Blue. Figure out your best move. Can you reach a subgoal that *must* lead to a win? Remember to watch out for threats from your opponent, Red!

Your best moves are as follows:

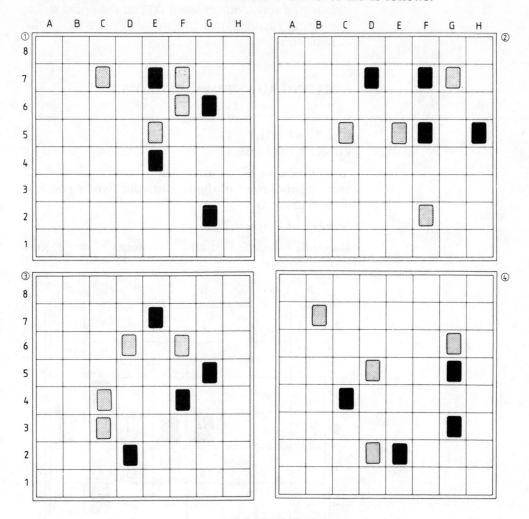

1. Play at F4, threatening four in a row along column F and on the diagonal in the upper left direction from F4.

2. Play at D4, threatening two diagonal rows of four (at E3 and F6).

3. By playing at C6, you threaten four in a row at E6 and C5. But Red already has a threat going. You must be on the defense now to survive. Play at E3.

4. Here you can fake a threat in one place, while developing a real threat somewhere else. Do you see

how? Play at D3. Red must play at D4 to stop your four in a row along column D. You then play at E4, creating two diagonal threats (at C6 and F5) at the same time.

## CREATING ROWS BY PLACING ONLY

### SM 17–1 (HL)
**RULES OF THE GAME**

*Aim of the Game*: To form as many horizontal, vertical, and diagonal rows of three, four, and five as possible with your cards.

*Number of Players*: Two.

*Materials Needed*: Red and blue decks of cards; grid 8×8.

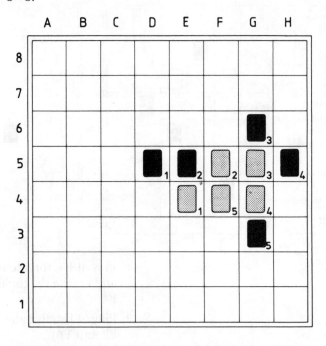

*How to Play*: Players alternate turns, one using the red deck, the other the blue. On each turn a player places one card on an empty square of the grid. After the first, each card placed on the grid must be adjacent horizontally, vertically, or diagonally to any card already there.

The game continues until all the squares on the grid are filled, or until both players agree there are no more opportunities to make three or more in a row.

*Scoring*: Each player receives one point for each three in a row, two points for each four in a row, and three points for each five in a row. The highest total wins.

This game gives you the opportunity to practice some of the strategy skills you have learned in the last four games.

In the example shown in the game rules, Red begins by placing a card into D5, and Blue responds at E4. Red's next turn (E5) creates two in a row open at both ends. While Blue can only block one end (at F5), Red cannot now complete three in a row because the rules require that the next card be placed adjacent to F5. Red therefore closes Blue's two in a row at G6, but Blue threatens again at G5, eventually getting the first three in a row at E4, F4, G4. An actual game would continue further than shown.

## CREATING ROWS WITH CAPTURING

In the next game, getting three cards in a row is a means for capturing the other player's cards.

### SM 18–1 (HL)
#### RULES OF THE GAME

*Aim of the Game*: To capture all the other player's cards by forming horizontal and vertical rows of three with your own cards.

*Number of Players*: Two

*Materials Needed*: 12 red and 12 blue cards; 6×6 grid.

*How to Play*: Players alternate turns, one player using the red cards, the other the blue cards.

*Phase I*: On each turn a player places one card face down in any empty square.

*Phase II*: When all 24 cards are placed on the grid, on each turn a player moves one card horizontally or vertically to an adjacent empty square. If a move connects exactly three of a player's cards in a straight horizontal or vertical line, the player chooses any one of the other player's cards to remove. A player who is blocked from moving loses a turn.

The game ends when one player is down to just two cards. That player loses.

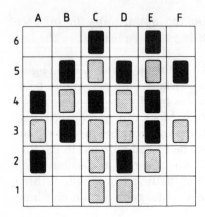

Let's go over a play-by-play example between two players, Red and Blue, from the point shown at the left. The last of the 24 cards has just been placed on the grid by Blue, and it is Red's turn to move. Notice that Blue already has three in a vertical row (at C1, C2, C3), but this does not entitle Blue to remove one of Red's cards because the row was created during Phase I (placing) and not during Phase II (moving).

Red moves from D5 to D6, creating a row at C6, D6, E6, and removes a blue card from C5:

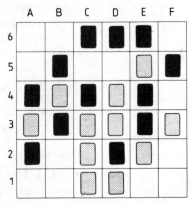

Blue moves from E2 to E1, creating a row at C1, D1, E1, and removes a red card from B3:

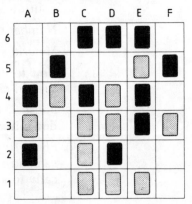

Now Red moves from B5 to C5, creating a row at C4, C5, C6, and removes a blue card from D4.

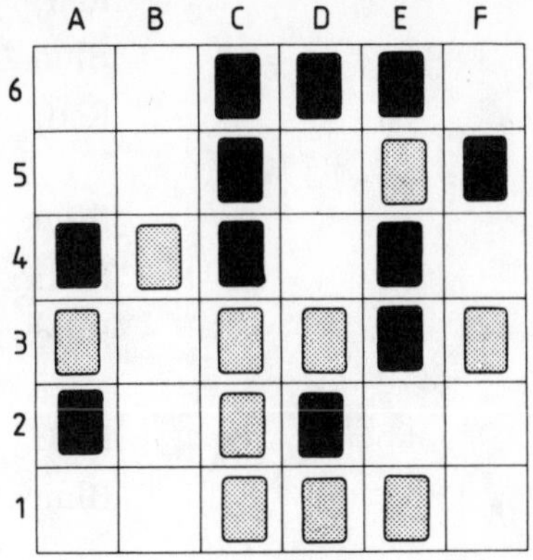

If Blue now moved from B4 to B3, it would create a row of *four* (A3, B3, C3, D3), which would *not* entitle Blue to remove a red card. So Blue moves from A3 to B3, creating a row of exactly three, and removes a red card from D2.

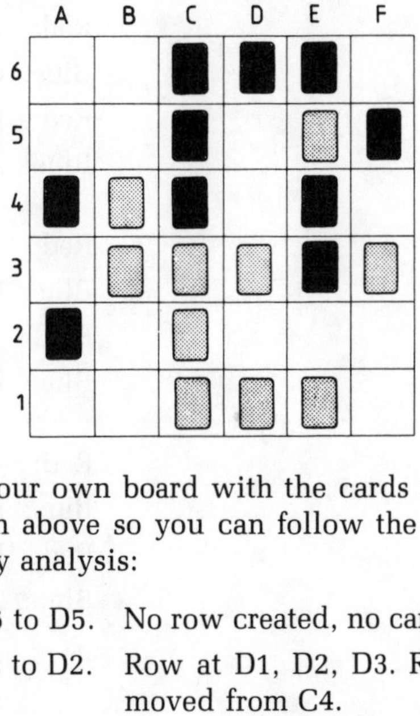

Set up your own board with the cards in the positions shown above so you can follow the rest of this play-by-play analysis:

Red:  D6 to D5.  No row created, no card removed.

Blue:  C2 to D2.  Row at D1, D2, D3. Red card removed from C4.

Red:  D5 to D6.  Row at C6, D6, E6. Blue card removed from D2.

Blue:  C1 to C2.  No row created.

Red:  C6 to B6.  No row created.

Blue: C2 to C1.   Row at C1, D1, E1. Red card removed from D6.

Red:   B6 to B5.

Blue: B3 to B2.

Red:   A4 to A5.   Row at A5, B5, C5. Blue card removed from C3.

Blue: D1 to D2.

Red:   C5 to C4.

Blue: E1 to D1.   Row at D1, D2, D3. Red card removed from C4.

Red:   E4 to D4.

Blue: C1 to C2.   Row at B2, C2, D2. Red card removed from D4.

Red:   E6 to D6.

Blue: D3 to C3.

Red:   D6 to D5.

Blue: C3 to B3.   Row at B2, B3, B4. Red card removed from B5.

Red:   E3 to E4.

Blue: C2 to C3.

Red:   D5 to D4.

Blue: D2 to D3.   Row at B3, B4, B5. Red card removed from E4.

Red:   A2 to A3.

Blue: B2 to A2.

Red:   A3 to A4.

Blue: A2 to B2.   Row at B2, B3, B4. Red card removed from A5.

Red:   F5 to F4.

Blue: B3 to B2.

Red:   F4 to E4.

Blue: A3 to B3.   Row at B3, C3, D3 and at B2, B3, B4 at the same time! But Blue is only entitled to remove one red card. Red card from D4.

At this point Red, with only two cards left, cannot form a row of three. Blue wins.

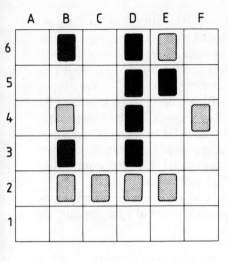

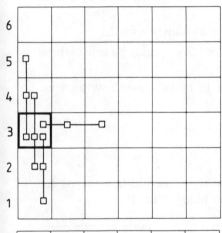

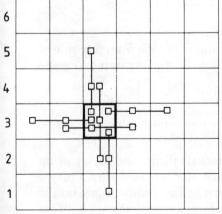

To be sure that you understand the rules before you begin playing, let's look at two situations that might occur in a game. And remember that you can remove one of your opponent's cards when your move has just connected exactly three of your cards in a straight horizontal or vertical row. First, in the situation at the left, it is Red's turn to move. Red already has a row of four at D3, D4, D5, D6. By moving from D3 to C3, Red creates a row of exactly three at D4, D5, D6 and is now entitled to remove one blue card. Second, if Red decides to remove the blue card at E2, Blue would then have a row of exactly three at B2, C2, D2. But Blue would *not* then be entitled to remove a red card, because the row was not created by Blue's own move.

Now that you understand the rules, play some games, seeing what strategic principles you can develop for the game before you read further. Note that certain strategic principles apply to Phase I of the game, placing your cards on the board. One general point is that you should plan to place your cards in good strategic positions, even though these positions do not lead directly toward getting lines of three in a row. It's better to place your cards in the *center* of the grid, rather than on the edges. Then you have more opportunities to get three in a line. A card placed at A3 (at the left) can be part of *four* different rows; a card placed at C3 (one of the four central squares) can be part of *six* different rows. From the central squares, you are also in a better position to move in any direction to block your opponent from getting a row of three.

See what other strategic principles you can develop for placing your cards during Phase I.

During Phase II you have two different kinds of decisions to make:

1. Where to move your cards.

2. After you create a row of three, which of your opponent's cards to remove.

These decisions deal more with *tactics* than *strategy*. Let's look more closely at them.

On the first point, try to arrange your cards so you can move one of them back and forth, creating a row on

|   | A | B | C | D | E | F |
|---|---|---|---|---|---|---|
| 6 |   |   |   |   |   | ▦ |
| 5 |   |   |   |   |   | ▦ |
| 4 |   |   |   |   |   | ▦ |
| 3 |   |   |   | ▦ | ▦ |   |
| 2 |   |   |   |   | ▦ | ▦ |
| 1 |   | ▦ | ▦ | ▦ |   |   |

each move. For example, in the situation on the left, Red can move a card from F4 to F3, creating a row at D3, E3, F3. Then, on the next move, Red can go back from F3 to F4, creating a row at F4, F5, F6. Red can continue going back and forth in this way, creating a row on each turn unless Blue interferes by blocking F3 or by removing one of Red's cards. In the same situation, Blue can move the card at D1 to D2, creating a row at D2, E2, F2. On the next move, Blue can then move back to D1, creating a row at B1, C1, D1, continuing back and forth unless Red interferes.

On the second point, you may have different sub-goals in mind when you remove one of your opponent's cards. You may want:

1. to destroy a back-and-forth situation like the one we have just described,
2. to isolate some of your opponent's cards,
3. to prevent your opponent from making a row of three on the next move, or
4. to give yourself room to make a new row on your next move.

## COMPLETING A PATH

In this game, a row that may "bend" is a means for building a path from one place to another.

---

### SM 19–1 (ML)
**RULES OF THE GAME**

*Aim of the Game:* To complete a path from one side of the grid to the opposite side by placing or moving one card at a time.

*Number of Players:* Two.

*Materials Needed:* Twelve red and twelve blue cards; 6×6 grid.

*How to Play:* Players alternate turns, one player using the red cards, the other the blue. On each turn a player places one card face down in any empty square on the grid. Each player tries to form a complete path with his or her cards from left to right side, or from top to bottom. Each card in the path must connect horizontally or vertically with the other cards in the path, but the cards may be put into the path in any order.

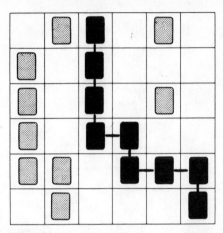

Example of winning path

If no path is formed when all the cards have been placed on the grid, the game enters the second phase. Players continue to alternate turns; on each turn a player moves one card horizontally or vertically to an empty adjacent square. The game ends when one player completes a path from left to right or from top to bottom.

# 4

# Strategy Games
# of Conflict

# REMOVING BY SANDWICHING

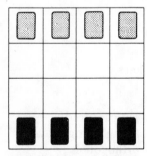

Starting position

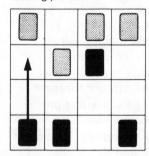

Example of
a capture

## SC 1–1 (LL)
### RULES OF THE GAME

*Aim of the Game*: To capture all of your opponent's cards but one by "sandwiching" them, or to block them all from moving.

*Number of Players*: Two.

*Materials Needed*: Two decks of cards; 4×4 grid.

*Preparation*: Four red and four blue cards are placed face down in the positions shown at the left.

*How to Play*: Player *A* uses the red deck, player *B* the blue. Players alternate turns, moving one card at a time. A card can be moved any number of squares horizontally or vertically, without jumping over another card. If a move "sandwiches" an opponent's card horizontally or vertically, the opponent's card is removed.

A card that is moved *into* a sandwich is not removed, unless the opponent moves one "slice of bread" away and then back.

The game ends when a player captures all but one of the opponent's cards, or blocks them all from moving.

## SC 1–2 (ML)

Same as SC 1–1, but with a 5×5 grid. Player *A* starts with five red cards in row 1, and Player *B* starts with five blue cards in row 5.

## SC 1–3 (ML)

Same as SC 1–1, but with a 6×6 grid. Player *A* starts with six red cards in row 1, and Player *B* starts with six blue cards in row 6.

---

Here's an example of how a game of SC 1–1 might go:

| *Red* | *Blue* | *Red* | *Blue* |
|---|---|---|---|
| 1. B1–B3 | C4–C3 | 5. A1–B1 | A4–B4 |
| 2. D1–D3 (captures) | B4–C4 | 6. A3–A4 | D4–C4 |
| 3. C1–C3 | A4–A2 | 7. D3–D4 | B4–B2 |
| 4. B3–A3 (captures) | C4–A4 | 8. C3–B3 (captures, wins) | |

## REVERSING BY SANDWICHING

---

## SC 2–1 (LL)

### RULES OF THE GAME

*Aim of the Game*: To make the majority of the cards on the grid yours by outflanking and overturning your opponent's cards.

*Number of Players*: Two.

*Materials Needed*: Deck of cards; 5×5 grid.

*Preparation*: Two face-up and two face-down cards are placed in the positions shown.

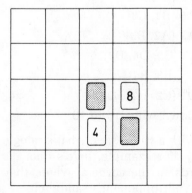

*How to Play*: Players alternate turns, one placing a face-up card on an empty square of the grid, the other a face-down card. Each card placed must form one end of a "sandwich" of one or more of the opponent's cards, either horizontally, vertically, or diagonally. The opponent's cards that are in the sandwich are then turned over on their other sides, to face the same way as the two "slices of bread." The card that has been placed may form more than one sandwich at the same time, but it must be the "piece of bread" for each sandwich so formed. A player who cannot form a sandwich loses a turn.

The game ends when all the squares are covered with cards, or when both players are unable to place a card. At that point the player with more cards facing his or her way (up or down) wins.

## SC 2–2 (ML)

Same as SC 2–1, but with a 7×7 grid, instead of 5×5. Start with face-up cards at D4 and E3 and face-down cards at D3 and E4, instead of in the positions shown.

---

Here is an example of how a game of SC 2–1 might begin. After we tell the location of each player's move, we show in parentheses the locations of the "sandwiched" cards that get turned over as a result of that move. Set up your grid so that you can follow this sample:

|     | *Up*           | *Down*              |
|-----|----------------|---------------------|
| 1.  | C4 (C3)        | B2 (C2)             |
| 2.  | E1 (D2)        | C5 (C3, C4)         |
| 3.  | A2 (B2, C2)    | A1 (B2)             |
| 4.  | B4 (C3)        | E2 (C2, D2, D3)     |

(Note: C3 is now sandwiched between C2 and C4, but it is not in a direct line with E2, the card that was just placed, so it is not turned over.)

5. E3 (D3, E2)

(Note: B2, C2, and D2 are now sandwiched between A2 and E2, but they are not in a direct line with E3, the card that was just placed, so they are not turned over.)

|     | *Up*              | *Down*                 |
|-----|-------------------|------------------------|
|     | . . .             | D4 (C3, D3)            |
| 6.  | B3 (C3, D3)       | A5 (B4, C3)            |
| 7.  | D5 (C4, D4)       | A3 (A2, B3)            |
| 8.  | C1 (C2, C3, D2)   | E5 (C3, D4, D5)        |
| 9.  | A4 (B3, B4)       | B5 (B3, B4)            |
| 10. | E4 (D4)           | D1 (C2, D2, D3, D4)    |
| 11. | B1 (C2, D3)       | Down wins, 15 to 10.   |

Play several games with a friend. See what strategic principles you develop. For example, here's one: It's good to have your cards in the corners, where they cannot become part of your opponent's sandwich.

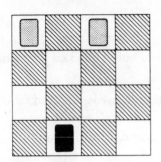

Starting position

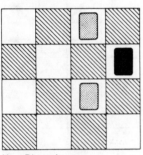

How Blue wins
by blocking

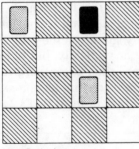

How Red wins
by blocking

## SC 3–1 (LL)
### RULES OF THE GAME

*Aim of the Game*: For Blue, to block the red card from moving diagonally. For Red, to reach the top side of the grid by moving diagonally.

*Number of Players*: Two.

*Materials Needed*: Two blue cards, one red card; 4×4 grid.

*Preparation*: Cards are placed face down on the squares shown:

*How to Play*: Player *A* uses the red deck, player *B* the blue deck. Players alternate turns, with red beginning. Red can move diagonally in any direction to an adjacent empty square. Blue can move diagonally only forwards (toward row 1) to an adjacent empty square. All cards move only on the white squares. Game continues until the blue cards completely block the red card from moving (Blue wins), or until the red card reaches row 4 (Red wins).

## SC 3–2 (ML)
Same as SC 3–1, but blue starts with *four* cards on the gray squares of row 8 of an 8×8 grid, instead of two cards in row 4 of a 4×4 grid. Red wins if the red card reaches row 8.

Here's how a game of SC 3–1 might go:

| Red | Blue |
|-----|------|
| 1. B1–C2 | A4–B3 |
| 2. C2–D3 | B3–C2 |

Red is blocked and cannot move; Blue wins.

143

## SC 4–1 (HL)
### RULES OF THE GAME

*Aim of the Game*: For Blue, to block the red card from moving. For Red, to avoid being blocked for 21 moves.

*Number of Players*: Two.

*Materials Needed*: Five blue cards, one red card; 4×4 grid.

*Preparation*: Cards are placed face down on the squares shown.

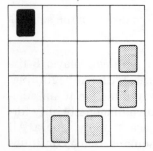

Starting position

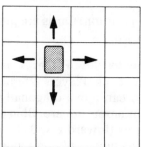

How Blue moves

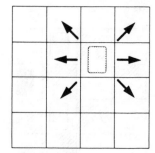

How Red moves

*How to Play*: Player *A* uses the red deck, Player *B* the blue deck. Players alternate turns. Red begins. Red can move either horizontally or diagonally, but not vertically, to an adjacent empty square on the grid. Blue can move either horizontally or vertically, but not diagonally, to an adjacent empty square on the grid. Game continues until the blue cards completely block the red card from moving (Blue wins), or until Red's 21st move (Red wins).

## TAKING ONE OR TWO FROM SEVEN TO TEN

In each of this group of games, the players compete to be the one who *places* the last card, *takes* the last card, or, in some cases, the one who *avoids* taking the last card. In most of these games, a simple strategy based on setting up subgoals will enable you to win. Sometimes thinking backwards from the winning position helps you set up the right subgoals. In one game *no* simple strategy works, and in another a very simple but suprising strategy works.

---

## SC 5–1 (LL)
**RULES OF THE GAME**

*Aim of the Game*: To take the last card by taking one or two from a group on each turn.

*Number of Players*: Two.

*Materials Needed*: Ten cards.

*Preparation*: From seven to ten cards (Player *A* chooses exactly how many) are spread out on the grid.

*How to Play*: Players alternate turns. On each turn a player must remove either one or two cards. Player who removes the last card wins.

## SC 5–2a (ML)
Same as SC 5–1, but each player takes one, two, or three away from ten to fifteen cards, instead of taking one or two away from seven to ten cards.

## SC 5–2b (ML)
Same as SC 5–1, but each player takes one, two, three, or four away from ten to fifteen cards, instead of taking one or two away from seven to ten cards.

## SC 5–2c (ML)
Same as SC 5–1, but each player takes from one to five away from ten to fifteen cards, instead of taking one or two away from seven to ten cards.

## SC 5–2d (ML)
Same as SC 5–1, but each player takes two to four away from ten to fifteen cards, instead of taking one or two away from seven to ten cards.

## SC 5–2e (ML)
Same as SC 5–1, but each player takes two to five away from ten to fifteen cards, instead of taking one or two away from seven to ten cards.

Suppose the game begins with seven cards, and you go first.

You take one, and six remain.

Your opponent takes two, and four remain.

You take one, three remain.

Your opponent takes one, two remain.

You take both.

You have taken the last card, and you win. But was this an accident? Could you win every time? What is the strategy here?

Play the game several times starting each time with seven cards, and then several times with eight, nine, and ten cards. Do you now see a strategy for winning all the time?

Toward the end of a game, if you are the player to leave just three cards, you can always force a win. If the other player takes one, you take two; if the other player takes two, you take one. This means that leaving exactly three cards is a subgoal for you. How can you be sure of reaching this subgoal? Earlier in the game, if you are the player who leaves exactly six cards, you can always force the situation so that you are also the player who leaves exactly three cards. Here's how: When six are left, if the other player takes two, you take one; if the other player takes one, you take two. Leaving exactly six cards, then, is also a subgoal for you.

In this same way, if you begin with more cards, leaving exactly nine, twelve, fifteen, eighteen, or any multiple of three becomes a subgoal too. For example, if the game starts with ten cards and you go first, you can take one, leaving nine. You have reached your first subgoal, and if you continue with your strategy, you must win.

In general, then, no matter how many cards you start with, divide the beginning number of cards by three, and take as many as there are in the remainder. This will get you to one of the subgoals. If there is no remainder, or if there is but you don't go first, you can hope that the other player doesn't know the strategy. At your first opportunity, take the number of cards necessary to reach one of the subgoals.

Why does this strategy work? When you leave exactly three, you create a situation where your opponent *cannot* win on the next turn because there is one more to take than a player is allowed to take. But *you* can win on your next turn no matter what your opponent does, because *three* is the sum of *one*, the minimum number of cards a player may take, and *two*, the maximum number of cards a player may take. If your opponent takes the minimum, you take the maximum. If your opponent takes the maximum, you take the minimum.

If you know why this strategy works, you will know how to adjust the strategy when the rules change. Let's now look at a game of SC 5–2a that begins with ten cards, and you go first:

You take two, and eight remain.

Your opponent takes three, and five remain.

You take one, four remain.

Your opponent takes one, three remain.

You take all three, and win.

......................

But was this an accident? Could you win every time? What is the strategy here?

Play the game several times starting each time with ten cards, and then several times with eleven, twelve, thirteen, fourteen, and fifteen cards. Do you now see a strategy for winning all the time?

Toward the end of a game, if you are the player to leave just four cards, you can always force a win. If the other player takes one, you take three; if the other player takes two, you take two; if the other player takes three, you take one.

This means that leaving exactly four cards is a subgoal for you. How can you be sure of reaching this subgoal? Earlier in the game, if you are the player who leaves exactly eight cards, you can always force the situation so that you are also the player who leaves exactly four cards. Here's how: When eight are left, if the other player takes one, you take two; if the other player takes two, you take two; if the other player takes three, you take one.

Leaving exactly eight cards, then, is also a subgoal for you. In the same way, if you begin with more cards, leaving exactly twelve, sixteen, twenty, or any multiple of four becomes a subgoal too. For example, if the game starts with ten cards and you go first, you can take two, leaving eight. Having reached your first subgoal, if you continue with your strategy, you must win. In general, no matter how many cards you start with, divide the beginning number of cards by four, and take as many as there are in the remainder. This gets you to one of the subgoals. If there is no remainder, or if there is but you don't go first, you can hope that the other player doesn't know the strategy. At your first opportunity, take the number of cards necessary to reach one of the subgoals.

Why does this strategy work? When you leave exactly four, you create a situation in which your opponent *cannot* win on the next turn because there is one more to take than a player is allowed to take. But *you* can win on your next turn no matter what your opponent does, because *four* is the sum of *one*, the minimum number of cards a player may take, and *three*, the maximum number of cards a player may take. If your opponent takes the minimum, you take the maximum. If your opponent takes the maximum, you take the minimum. If your opponent takes two, between the minimum and maximum, you do the same.

If you know why this strategy works, you will know how to adjust the strategy when the rules change. Can you figure out the subgoals for SC 5–2b, c, d, and e? Here they are:

b. . . . 20, 15, 10, 5.  c. . . . 24, 18, 12, 6.
d. . . . 24, 18, 12, 6.  e. . . . 28, 21, 14, 7.

See if you can use this same sort of analysis to find a winning strategy in the next few games.

## TAKING ONE OR FOUR FROM TWENTY: THREE PLAYERS

### SC 6–1 (ML)
#### RULES OF THE GAME

*Aim of the Game*: To take the last card by taking one or four from a group of cards on each turn.

*Number of Players*: Three.

*Materials Needed*: Deck of cards; 4×5 grid.

*Preparation*: Place one card face down in each of the twenty squares of the grid.

*How to Play*: The three players alternate turns. On each turn a player must take one or four cards. The player who takes the last card wins.

Play this game a few times to get familiar with it. It is a curious game. It doesn't matter whether you or anyone else takes one or four cards, on the first turn or on any other turn. The second player always wins. The winning strategy is to be the second player!

After each round (each of the three players taking one turn), a total of either three $(1+1+1)$, six $(1+1+4)$, nine $(1+4+4)$, or twelve $(4+4+4)$ will have been taken away. This means that after each round, a number divisible by three will have been taken away. Because we start with twenty, the only outcomes we can get after one round are seventeen, fourteen, eleven, and eight. In later rounds we could also wind up with five or two.

When we reach two at the end of a round, the second player clearly must win. The first player takes one card, and the second player takes the last.

When we reach five at the end of a round, again the second player must win. If the first player takes four, the second player takes the last and wins. If the first player takes one, the second player takes four and wins.

## SC 7–1 (ML)

### RULES OF THE GAME

*Aim of the Game:* To reach the total card value of 31 by turning cards face down one at a time.

*Number of Players:* Two.

*Materials Needed:* Deck of cards; 4×6 grid.

*Preparation:* The aces through 6s (1–6) in the four suits are placed face up in the grid as shown.

*How to Play:* Players alternate turns. On each turn a player turns one card face down. A count is kept of the total value of all cards turned face down (ace=1). The player who turns down the card that reaches exactly 31 wins. A player who goes over 31 loses.

| 1 | 1 | 1 | 1 |
| 2 | 2 | 2 | 2 |
| 3 | 3 | 3 | 3 |
| 4 | 4 | 4 | 4 |
| 5 | 5 | 5 | 5 |
| 6 | 6 | 6 | 6 |

From the analysis of SC 5–2a, can you find a winning strategy for this game? The minimum you can turn down is 1, the maximum is 6. The sum of minimum and maximum is 7. So no matter what your opponent does, you can make the total turned down in one play by your opponent and one play by you equal to 7. So your final subgoal, 8 points away from 431, is 234, The subgoals before 24 are 3, 10, and 17.

## TAKING FROM ROWS OF THREE, FIVE, AND SEVEN

In SC 5–2a, you had to take away one, two, or three cards from a group, trying to be the one who takes the last card of the group. This game involves three groups of cards, and you can take as many cards away as you want from any one of the groups. You try to be the one to take away the last card of all the groups.

## SC 8–1 (HL)

### RULES OF THE GAME

*Aim of the Game:* To take the last card by taking any number of cards from one of three rows.

*Number of Players:* Two

*Materials Needed*: Deck of cards; 3×7 grid.

*Preparation*: Place face down in the grid three cards in the top row, five cards in the middle row, and seven cards in the bottom row:

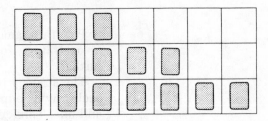

*How to Play*: Players alternate turns. On each turn a player must take as many cards in one row as he or she wishes.

---

Here's how a game might go.

First player takes four from bottom row, leaving

Second player takes five from middle row, leaving

First player takes one from top row, leaving

Second player takes one from bottom row, leaving

First player takes two from bottom row, leaving

Second player takes two from top row, and wins!

Play this game a several times. See if you can arrive at a strategy for always winning before you read further. . . .

The strategy in this game is to think of the cards in each row as bunched together in groups of four, two, and one. Think of the *biggest* groups possible for each row. For example, at the beginning you would think of the cards grouped as shown in situation a. You would not group the bottom row as shown in layout b, because a group of four is possible.

a.

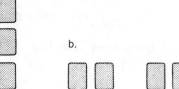

b.

Next, see if you can pair up in your mind every group in one row with a group in another row. At the beginning of the game you could group them as in situation c. One card in the bottom row is unpaired. If you had grouped it together with the single card in the middle row, then there would be an unpaired card in the top row. If you had grouped together single cards in the top and bottom rows, there would be an unpaired card in the middle row.

c.

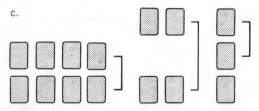

*Your subgoal on each move is always to leave every group in one row paired with a group of the same size in another row.* So, if you have the first turn, you could take away a card from either the top, middle, or bottom row to reach this subgoal. Then, *once you reach a subgoal, you can always continue to reach other subgoals on every turn until you win.*

Let's look again at our example. The first player did not use the winning strategy, the second player did.

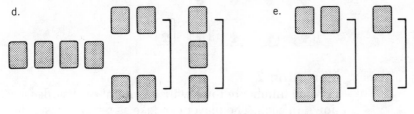

d.

e.

When the first player took four cards from the bottom row, the second player regrouped the cards mentally, as shown in situation d. The group of four in the middle row was unpaired with another group. There was also an unpaired card in either the top, middle, or bottom row, depending on how you look at it. The second player, who could take cards only from one row, took all five in the middle row, eliminating the unpaired group of four and the unpaired group of one in one stroke. This move left situation e.

When the first player took a single card from the top row, an unpaired group of one was left in the bottom row, as in situation f. The second player removed this unpaired card, leaving situation g. When the first player then took both cards in the bottom row, leaving an unpaired group of two, the second player removed this group and won.

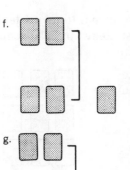

f.

g.

## Variation 1

Shuffle the cards, and take the first fifteen or so. Deal them out on the grid face up in the shuffled order. Instead of taking as many cards from one *row* as a player wants, each player takes as many cards as he or she wants from one *suit* on each turn. It will be harder for your opponent to figure out the strategy. It may also be harder for you to group the cards in your mind.

For example, if the cards are dealt out as shown at the left on the next page, you must group them in your head in "rows" as shown on the right.

## Variation 2

Use any number of rows, with any number of cards face down in each. The player can take as many cards as he or she wants from any row. Same strategy!

## Variation 3

Change the aim of the game: to *avoid* taking the last card. The same basic strategy applies except at the end of the game. For example:

The first player takes
four from the bottom row:

The second player takes
five from middle row:

The first player takes
one from top row:

The second player takes
one from bottom row:

The first player takes
two from bottom row:

The second player takes one, leaving one, which first player must take. The second player wins!

## MOVE AND BLOCK

### SC 9–1 (HL)
**RULES OF THE GAME**

*Aim of the Game*: To be the last player to move along the columns of an 8×8 grid.

*Number of Players*: Two

*Materials Needed*: Eight red and eight blue cards; 8×8 grid.

*Preparation*: The red cards are placed face down on the top row, the blue cards face down on the bottom row.

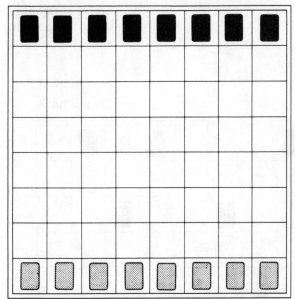

*How to Play*: Players alternate turns. One player controls the blue cards, the other the red cards. On each turn, a player may move any of his or her cards any number of squares vertically toward the opponent's card in the same column. When two cards are on adjacent squares in the same column, neither card can move further. The last player to move one of his or her cards wins.

Let's see how a game might go. Set the starting position upon your own grid, so you can follow this play-by-play analysis. Red goes first.

| | | | |
|---|---|---|---|
| 1. Red | C6 | 8. Blue | C5 (column C now blocked) |
| 2. Blue | D2 | 9. Red | H4 |
| 3. Red | D3 (column D now blocked) | 10. Blue | G7 (column G now blocked) |
| 4. Blue | E7 (column E now blocked) | 11. Red | B4 |
| 5. Red | F6 | 12. Blue | F2 |
| 6. Blue | A6 | 13. Red | H3 |
| 7. Red | B6 | | |

The situation is shown below. What strategy can win for Blue? Have you recognized that this game is just like Variation 2 of Game SC 9–1? There are eight *columns* (instead of rows) of six empty *squares* (instead of *cards*) at the beginning. Your subgoal is to leave every group in one column paired with a group the same size in another column. In this situation, these groups exist:

| | | | |
|---|---|---|---|
| Column A: | 1 | Column F: | 1 and 2 |
| Column B: | 2 | Column G: | 1 |

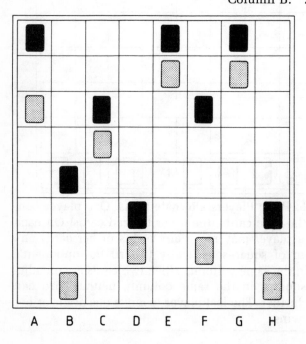

A     B     C     D     E     F     G     H

Blue can win by closing up the gap in Column A or Column G, or by moving one square in Column F. That will leave two paired groups of two, and two paired groups of one.

## Variation 1

The aim is to *avoid* being the last to move.

### TAKE AND DISCONNECT

## SC 10–1 (HL)
### RULES OF THE GAME

*Aim of the Game*: To take the last card by taking cards that are horizontally or vertically adjacent to each other.

*Number of Players*: Two

*Materials Needed*: Deck of cards; 4×4 grid.

*Preparation*: Place one card face down in each of the sixteen squares of the grid.

*How to Play*: The players alternate turns. On each turn a player may take as many adjacent cards as he or she wants from any horizontal row or vertical column. A player must take at least one card.

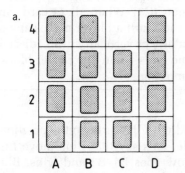

Suppose on the first turn a player has taken the card in C4, leaving situation a (to the left). The next player may take D2, D3, and D4 in one turn because they are in the same row and adjacent. Or the player may take A4 and B4 on the same turn, but not A4, B4, and D4, due to the gap between B4 and D4.

Suppose the second player does take D2, D3 and D4. We get the situation in b. The first player now takes A1, B1, C1 and D1, leaving situation c. The second player takes B2, and first player takes A2, A3, and A4, leaving situation d. The second player now takes B3 and C3, leaving two isolated cards at B4 and C2. The second player must now win: Whichever card the first player takes, the second player takes the other.

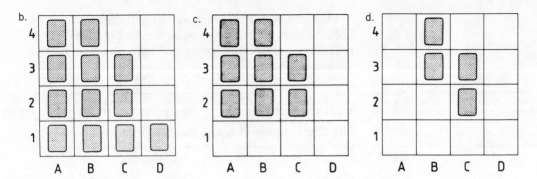

This can be a very fascinating game. No strategy is known that guarantees a win from the beginning in this game.

## BLOCKING BY MOVING

### SC 11–1 (LL)

**RULES OF THE GAME**

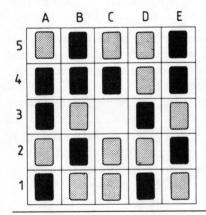

*Aim of the Game*: To block the other player's cards from moving on the grid.

*Number of Players*: Two

*Materials Needed*: Twelve red and twelve blue cards; 5×5 grid.

*How to Play*: Players alternate turns, one player using the red cards, the other player the blue. On each turn, a player places one card face up on any empty square on the grid except the center (C3). When all 24 cards are placed on the grid, on each turn a player moves any of his or her cards horizontally or vertically to an adjacent empty square. The game ends when one player blocks the other player from moving.

Set up your own grid with the cards in the positions shown. In our example, let's say that Blue move first from B3 to C3. Red now goes B4–B3 and wins. Blue cannot move. If Red had moved B2–B3, Blue could move C2–B2 and win.

Play a few games to see what strategic principles you can come up with; then read further. . . .

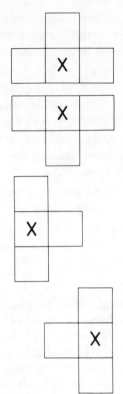

They way to win, of course, is to surround the empty square with your own cards. If the empty square is one of the nine central ones (B2, B3, B4, C2, C3, C4, D2, D3, or D4), then you need four of your cards to surround it. You need three of your cards to surround an empty square on the edge, and only two to surround an empty square in the corner.

In this game, as in SM 18–1, there is a strategy for *placing* your cards on the board, and a strategy for *moving* them. Regarding placement, you must place at least one card adjacent to the center if you move first. Otherwise you will lose on the first move! Regarding movement, you should try to move your cards into a "T" formation in any rotation. Think of these as "T" shapes. If you can maneuver the top of your T (marked with the "x") so that it is adjacent to the empty square when it's your turn to play, you can win. You just move the top of the "T" into the empty square, and you have it surrounded. As a defensive strategy, you should not let your opponent form "T" shapes, especially near the empty square.

## SOWING: FOUR SQUARES, TWO TOKENS IN EACH

In this group of games, the player chooses a *location* from which to take cards, and then "sows" them, one at a time, into other locations in a fixed order. These games are versions of *Mancala*, also known as *Wari*, which is many hundreds of years old and widely played in Africa, Asia, and the Caribbean.

## SC 12–1 (LL)
### RULES OF THE GAME

*Aim of the Game:* To get all the tokens that are initially in squares A through D into square E by moving them according to a "sowing" rule.

*Number of Players:* One

*Materials Needed:* Eight tokens; 1×5 grid.

*Preparation:* Place two tokens in each square A through D.

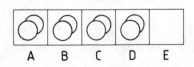

*How to Play*: Player takes the tokens from any square, and distributes them to the right, one token to a square. The squares are considered to be in a loop, where A is to the right of E.

1. If the last token goes into E, player selects any other square (except E) from which to take out and distribute tokens to the right, one token to a square.

2. If the last token goes into a square (other than E) that already has tokens, player takes all the tokens from that square to distribute as above.

3. If the last token goes into a square (other than E) that has no tokens in it, the player loses.

At any time a player is allowed to count how many tokens are in a square. If all eight tokens land in E, the player wins.

a.

| 2 | 0 | 3 | 3 | 0 |
|---|---|---|---|---|
| A | B | C | D | E |

b.

| 3 | 1 | 3 | 0 | 1 |
|---|---|---|---|---|
| A | B | C | D | E |

Here's how a game might go. The player takes two tokens from B and distributes them into C and D. (See situation a.) Since the last token landed in D, which already has tokens, the player continues by taking all three tokens out of D, and distributing them to E, A, and B. (See situation b.) The last token landed in B, which had no tokens, so the player loses.

Here's another example of how a game might go:

Start:

| 2 | 2 | 2 | 2 | 0 |
|---|---|---|---|---|
| A | B | C | D | E |

Player takes from C:

| 2 | 2 | 0 | 3 | 1 |
|---|---|---|---|---|
| A | B | C | D | E |

Last token landed in E, player chooses to take from A:

| 0 | 3 | 1 | 3 | 1 |
|---|---|---|---|---|
| A | B | C | D | E |

The last token landed in C, which had no tokens, so the player loses.

Now play the game by yourself, and see if you can come up with a winning strategy before you read further. . . .

Here is a winning strategy. To the left of each row, we tell you which square to take from:

| | A | B | C | D | E | |
|---|---|---|---|---|---|---|
| C | 2 | 2 | 2 | 2 | 0 | |
| D | 2 | 2 | 0 | 3 | 1 | |
| B | 3 | 3 | 0 | 0 | 2 | |
| C | 3 | 0 | 1 | 1 | 3 | |
| D | 3 | 0 | 0 | 2 | 3 | |
| A | 4 | 0 | 0 | 0 | 4 | |
| D | 0 | 1 | 1 | 1 | 5 | |
| B | 0 | 1 | 1 | 0 | 6 | |
| C | 0 | 0 | 2 | 0 | 6 | |
| D | 0 | 0 | 0 | 1 | 7 | |
| | 0 | 0 | 0 | 0 | 8 | win! |

## SOWING: EIGHT SQUARES, TWO TOKENS IN EACH

On your first turn in this game, you choose which square to take tokens from. Later you have a choice only when the last token lands in square E. But in the next game, you must choose on *each* turn which square to take the tokens from. You play against an opponent, and you use a larger grid.

## SC 13–1 (ML)
### RULES OF THE GAME

*Aim of the Game*: To capture more tokens than your opponent by moving according to a "sowing" rule.

*Number of Players*: Two

*Materials Needed*: Sixteen tokens; 2×6 grid, blocked off as shown.

*Preparation*: Two tokens are placed into each square, except for A2 and F1.

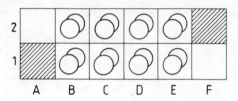

*How to Play*: The squares form a loop in this order: B1, C1, D1, E1, F1, E2, D2, C2, B2, A2, B1, and so on. Row 1 belongs to player *A*, row 2 to player *B*. The players alternate turns, beginning with player *A*.

On each turn a player takes all the tokens from any square of his or her row (except for A2 and F1) and distributes them counterclockwise, one token to a square, beginning with the next square. Tokens that land on A2 or F1 are never removed.

If the last token distributed lands on a square in the player's own row that is otherwise empty, the player captures all the tokens in the opposite square in the opponent's row. The captured tokens are placed into F1 by player *A* and into A2 by player *B*.

The game ends when one player has no more tokens in his or her row to play.

*Scoring*: Each player receives one point for each token the player has captured, minus one point for each token left in his or her row at the end of each game. The player with more points wins.

## SC 13–2 (HL)
Same as SC 13–1, but using a 2×8 grid and starting with three tokens in each square, except for A2 and H1, instead of a 2×6 grid with two tokens in each square, except for A2 and F1.

---

Here's an example of how a game of SC 13–1 might go. In each diagram we have underlined the square from which a player has chosen to take tokens:

| 1. | 0 | 2 | 2 | 2 | 2 |   |
|    |   | 2 | 2 | <u>2</u> | 2 | 0 |

| 6. | 1 | 0 | <u>3</u> | 0 | 0 |   |
|    |   | 1 | 0 | 2 | 4 | 5 |

| 2. | 0 | 2 | 2 | 2 | <u>2</u> |   |
|    |   | 2 | 2 | 0 | 3 | 1 |

| 7. | 2 | 1 | 0 | 0 | 0 |   |
|    |   | 2 | 0 | <u>2</u> | 4 | 5 |

| 3. | 0 | 2 | 3 | 3 | 0 |   |
|    |   | <u>2</u> | 2 | 0 | 3 | 1 |

| 8. | 2 | <u>1</u> | 0 | 0 | 0 |   |
|    |   | 2 | 0 | 0 | 5 | 6 |

| 4. | 0 | <u>2</u> | 3 | 0 | 0 |   |
|    |   | 0 | 3 | 1 | 3 | 4 |

| 9. | <u>3</u> | 0 | 0 | 0 | 0 |   |
|    |   | 2 | 0 | 0 | 5 | 6 |

| 5. | 1 | 0 | 3 | 0 | 0 |   |
|    |   | 1 | <u>3</u> | 1 | 3 | 4 |

The game ends. Player *A* gets six points for the tokens he or she has captured, minus seven points for player *A*'s tokens left on the grid, for a total of minus one point. Player *B* gets three points for the tokens captured. Player B wins.

Get familiar with this game by playing it, and see what strategic principles you can develop.

## GO: LINEAR

In this group are versions of the game GO, which comes from Asia. In these games you capture your opponent's cards by surrounding them with your own. You also attempt to control certain squares by surrounding them with your cards.

---

## SC 14–1 (LL)
### RULES OF THE GAME

*Aim of the Game:* To place your cards in a row of squares so they surround both sides of more squares and capture more of your opponent's cards than your opponent does.

*Number of Players:* Two

*Materials Needed:* Four red and four blue cards; 1×5 grid.

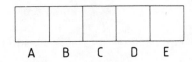

*How to Play*: Players alternate turns, one player using the red cards, the other player the blue. On each turn, a player places one card on an empty square. When an opponent's card or an opponent's group of adjacent cards is "sandwiched" between two of the player's cards or between one of the player's cards and the end of the grid, the opponent's sandwiched cards are captured and removed.

A player may not place his or her card into such a sandwich, unless doing so enables the player to remove one or both pieces of "bread" on that move.

A player may not place his or her card in a way that repeats the position that resulted from the player's previous move.

The game ends when all the cards have been placed once on the grid, or when neither player is able to or wishes to make further plays.

*Scoring*: Each player receives one point for each square under his or her control (surrounded by two of the player's cards, or one of the player's cards and the end of the grid), and one point for each of the opponent's cards that has been captured.

---

Here's how a game between Blue and Red might go. We will represent an empty square on the grid by –, a Blue by B, and a Red by R.

| | |
|---|---|
| – B – – – | On the first move, Blue places a card into square B. |
| – B R – – | Red places a card into square C. |
| – B – B – | The red card is surrounded and removed. |

At this point a red card cannot be played in square A because it would be between the left end of the grid and the blue card in square B. A red card cannot be played in C, because it would be between blue cards at B and D. A red card cannot be played at E, because it would be between the blue card at D and the right end of the grid. Red has no play to make, and Blue does not want to make a play. The game ends.

Blue receives three points for controlling the squares at A, C, and E, and one point for the captured red card, for a total of four points. Red has no points. Blue wins.

Here's another example:

```
– B – – –
– B – R –
– B B R –
R – – R –     Two blue cards captured.
R – B R –
R R – R –     One blue card captured.
```

Blue now has nowhere to play, and Red doesn't want to play. (By playing, Red would just cut out one of the squares Red already controls.) The game ends. Red gets two points for controlling the squares at C and E, and three points for the captured blue cards, for a total of five. Blue has no points. Red wins.

Here's one more example.

```
– – B – –
– – B R –
– – B – B     Red card captured.
– R B – B
B – B – B     Another red card captured, looks
              like Blue wins.
– R B – B     Blue card captured.
```

Now Blue cannot play at A, because doing so would repeat the position that resulted from Blue's previous move (B – B – B). And Blue cannot play at D, because doing so would create a "Blue sandwich" with the blue cards on C, D, and E. So Blue must pass. Red now plays again.

```
– R – R –     Two blue cards captured.
```

Blue now has no place to play, and Red doesn't want to play. The game ends. Red controls three squares (A, C, and E) and has captured three blue cards, for a total of six points. Blue has captured two red cards for two points. Red wins after all!

Now play this game with a friend, and explore all the possibilities. Do you see which are the two most important squares to place your cards on? They are B and D.

## GO: TWO DIMENSIONS

This next game uses basically the same rules, but it expands the grid to two dimensions.

---

## SC 15–1 (ML)
### RULES OF THE GAME

*Aim of the Game*: To place your cards on a grid so they surround all sides of more squares and to capture more of your opponent's cards than your opponent does.

*Number of Players*: Two.

*Materials Needed*: Thirteen red and thirteen blue cards; 4×4 grid.

*Preparation*: Each player is given thirteen cards of his or her own color.

*How to Play*: Players alternate turns. On each turn, a player places one card on an empty square. When an opponent's card, or an opponent's group of adjacent cards that are connected horizontally or vertically, is surrounded on all horizontally and vertically adjacent squares by the player's cards or by the player's cards and the edges of the grid, the opponent's surrounded card(s) are captured and removed.

A player may not place his or her card into such a surrounded position unless doing so enables the player to remove one or more of the surrounding cards on that move.

A player may not place his or her card in a way that repeats the position that resulted from the player's previous move.

The game ends when all the cards have been placed once on the grid, or when neither player is able to or wishes to make further plays.

*Scoring*: Each player receives one point for each square under his or her control (surrounded by the player's cards or by the player's cards and the edges of the grid) when the game ends, and one point for each of the opponent's cards that has been captured.

## SC 15–2 (ML)

Same as SC 15–1, except that each player is given eighteen cards, instead of thirteen, and the grid is 6×6 instead of 4×4.

## SC 15–3 (HL)

Same as SC 15–1, except that each player is given twenty-six cards, instead of thirteen, and the grid is 8×8 instead of 4×4.

Here's how a game of SC 15–1 might go.

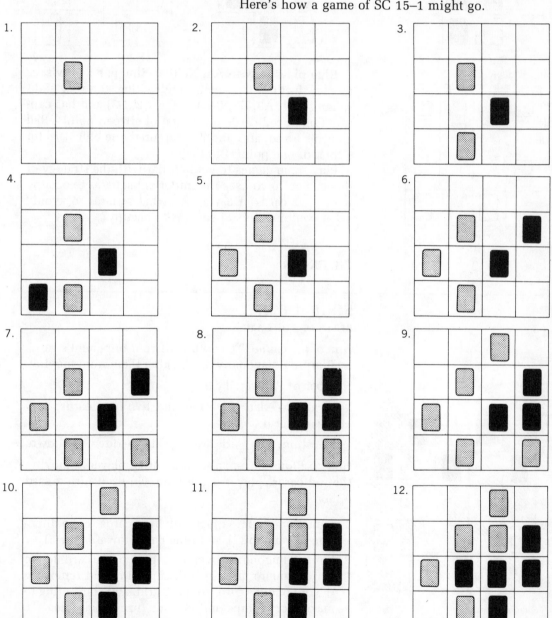

13.

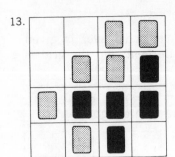

14.

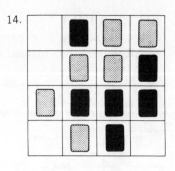

15.

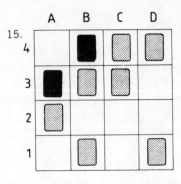

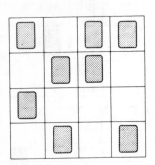

Blue plays now in A4. Neither Blue nor Red wishes to play further. The game ends. Blue controls eight squares (A1, A3, B2, B4, C1, C2, D2, D3) and has captured eight red cards for a total of sixteen points. Red controls no squares and has captured one blue card for a total of one point. Blue wins.

Play some games to get familiar with the strategy of this game. Do you see the important squares to occupy with your cards? Do you see what squares to avoid? What combinations of squares to occupy?

## CHECKERS

### SC 16–1 (LL)
#### RULES OF THE GAME

*Aim of the Game*: To capture all your opponent's cards by jumping diagonally or blocking them from moving.

*Number of Players*: Two

*Materials Needed*: Five red and five blue cards; 5×5 checkered grid.

*Preparation*: The cards are placed face down as shown.

*How to Play*: Players alternate turns, player *A* moving the red cards, player *B* the blue. On each turn a card either:

1. moves one square diagonally (red cards in the direction toward row 1 and blue cards toward row 5), or

2. jumps diagonally over an opponent's card to an empty square just beyond, capturing and removing the opponent's card from the grid, and continuing to make more jumps on the same turn if possible.

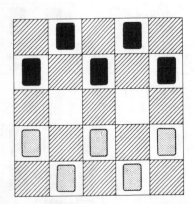

Starting position

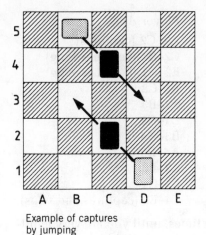

Example of captures
by jumping

A player *must* capture at every opportunity but may choose which capture to make if there is more than one possibility.

When a red card reaches row 1 or a blue card reaches row 5, it ends its turn, gets placed sideways (see Example in square B5), and is called a "king." A king moves and jumps like any other card, but in *any* diagonal direction.

The game ends when one player has captured or blocked from moving all the other player's cards. If at some point in the game both players agree this cannot happen, the game is a tie.

## SC 16–2 (ML)

Same as SC 16–1, but with an 8×8 grid instead of 5×5. Each player starts with twelve cards, placed on the white squares of rows 1–3 for Blue, and 6–8 for Red.

## SC 16–3 (ML)

Same as SC 16–2, but the goal is to have your opponent capture all *your* cards, instead of your capturing the opponent's cards.

---

Here's how a game of SC 16–1 might go:

| Player B: | Player A: |
|---|---|
| C2–D2 | E4–C2 (captures) |
| B1–D3 (captures) | D5–E4 |
| D1–C2 | C4–B3 |
| A2–C4 (captures) | A4–B3 |
| C2–A4 (captures, wins) | |

Can Blue (player B) always win by going first? Let's look at another game, where Red does something different on Red's second move.

| Player B: | Player A: |
|---|---|
| C2–D3 | E4–C2 (captures) |
| B1–D3 (captures) | A4–B3 |
| D3–E4 | B5–A4 |
| E2–D3 | C4–E2 (captures) |
| A2–C4 (captures) | D5–B3 (captures) |
| C4–D5 (becomes king) | B3–C2 |

| Player B: | Player A: |
|---|---|
| D1–B3 (captures) | A4–C2 (captures) |
| D5–C4 | C2–B1 (becomes king) |
| C4–D3 | E2–D1 (becomes king) |
| D3–C4 | B1–C2 |
| C4–B5 | C2–B3 |
| B5–A4 | D1–C2 |
| A4–B5 | B3–A4 |
| B5–C4 | A4–B5 |
| C4–D5 | C2–B3 |
| D5–E4 | B5–C4 |
| E4–D3 | C4–E2 (captures and wins). |

Play this game many times, until you are very familiar with it. See what strategic principles you can come up with.

## CHECKERS: THE "LONG" KING MOVES

### SC 17–1 (HL)
**RULES OF THE GAME**

*Aim of the Game*: To capture all your opponent's cards by jumping diagonally or blocking them from moving, with "long" jumps allowed by kings.

*Number of Players*: Two

*Materials Needed*: Twelve red and twelve blue cards; 8×8 grid.

*Preparation*: The cards are placed face down as shown.

*How to Play*: Players alternate turns, player A moving the red cards, player B the blue. On each turn a card either:

1. moves one square diagonally (red cards in the direction toward row 1 and blue cards toward row 8), or

2. jumps diagonally over an opponent's card to an empty square just beyond, capturing and removing the opponent's card from the grid, and continuing to make more jumps on the same turn if possible.

A player *must* capture at every opportunity but may choose which capture to make if there is more than one possibility.

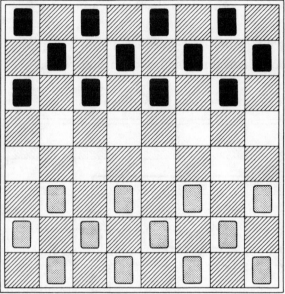

Starting position

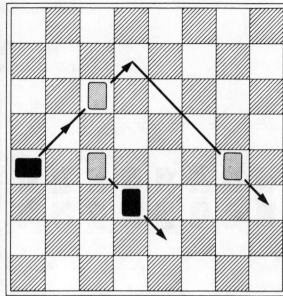

Examples of captures
by jumping

When a red card reaches row 1 or a blue card reaches row 8, it ends its turn, gets placed sideways (see Examples of Capturing by Jumping, right), and is called a "king." A king moves like any other card, but in *any* diagonal direction. It can capture an opponent's card *anywhere* on its diagonal by jumping to the empty square just beyond it, if there are no intervening cards on that diagonal, and continuing to make further jumps on the same turn if possible.

The game ends when one player has captured or blocked from moving all the other player's cards. If at some point in the game both players agree this cannot happen, the game is a tie.

## CHECKERS: ORTHOGONAL

### SC 18–1 (HL)
#### RULES OF THE GAME

*Aim of the Game*: To capture all your opponent's cards by jumping horizontally or vertically over them, or blocking them from moving, with "long" jumps allowed by kings.

*Number of Players*: Two

*Materials Needed*: Sixteen red and sixteen blue cards; 8×8 grid.

*Preparation*: The cards are placed face down as shown.

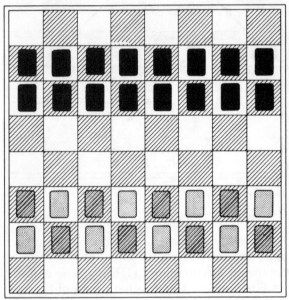

Starting position

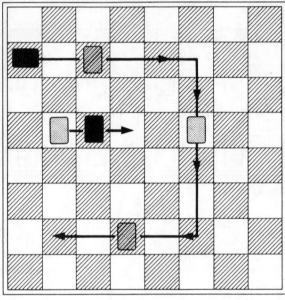

Examples of captures
by jumping

*How to Play*: Players alternate turns, player *A* moving the red cards, player *B* the blue. On each turn a card either:

1. moves one square *forward* (red cards toward row 1, and blue cards toward row 8) or *sideways*, or

2. *jumps* forward or sideways over an opponent's card to an empty square just beyond, capturing and removing the opponent's card from the grid, and continuing to make more jumps on the same turn if possible.

A player *must* capture at every opportunity but may choose which capture to make if there is more than one possibility.

When a red card reaches row 1 or a blue card reaches row 8, it ends its turn, gets placed sideways (see Examples of Capturing by Jumping, square A7), and is called a "king." A king moves *forward*, *backward*, or *sideways*, as many empty squares as it likes. It can capture an opponent's card *anywhere* in its own row or column by jumping to *any* square beyond it on the same column or row if there are no intervening cards. It can continue to make further jumps on the same turn if possible.

The game ends when one player has captured or blocked from moving all the other player's cards. If at some point in the game both players agree this cannot happen, the game is a tie.

---

## CHESS

Like checker games, chess can also be played with cards, and we will show you how. In fact, all the games so far in this chapter have led up to the game of chess. With this complex game, one of the world's greatest strategy games, you can greatly strengthen your "strategy muscle."

Some people think the game of chess is too complicated to learn and enjoy. It doesn't have to be so. We will employ the same progressive method we've used throughout the book to make chess easy and enjoyable for you to learn. Through simple games, you learn how each chess piece moves.

### The Chess Pieces

Each player has six different kinds of pieces: the king, queen, rook, knight, bishop, and pawn. Each kind of chess piece has its own move. You already have the set of cards with pictures of the kind of chess pieces that comes with this game system. If not, you can make them, or use ordinary playing cards to represent them, like this:

K = king      Q = queen
1 = rook      10 = bishop
7 = knight    2, 3 = pawn

The king moves one square horizontally, vertically, or diagonally in any direction, but it may *not* move into a square where it can be captured.

The *queen* moves horizontally, vertically, or diagonally as many squares as desired, in any direction, if no other piece gets in the way.

A *rook* moves horizontally or vertically as many squares as desired, if no other piece gets in the way.

A *bishop* moves diagonally as many squares as desired, in any direction, if no other piece gets in the way.

A *knight* moves to the next square up, down, left, or right (which need not be empty), then continues one square diagonally *away from* the starting square. The knight ends each move on a square of a different color than its starting square.

A king, queen, rook, bishop, or knight landing in a square occupied by an opponent's chess piece captures and removes it.

A *pawn* may either:

- move one square straight forward to an empty square (red pawns toward row 8, black pawns toward row 1), *or*
- move diagonally forward to an adjacent square occupied by an opposing piece, remove it from the grid, and occupy the square it was in.

Summary of How Each Chess Piece Moves.

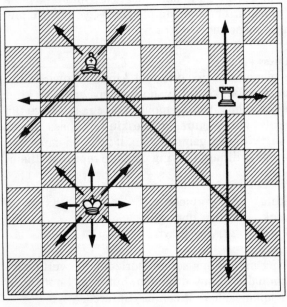
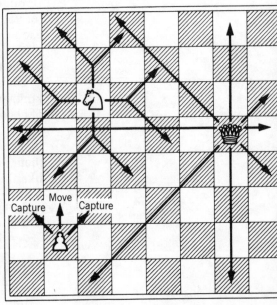

No chess piece may land in a square occupied by another piece of the same color.

Our strategy for the chapter is first to present the rules for the standard chess game, so you can see what we are leading up to. (You will want to skim this and return to it later.) Then we present a series of games, starting with very simple ones, that help you learn how each chess piece moves and that give you some basic strategy ideas for chess.

## THE STANDARD CHESS GAME

### SC 19–1 (HL)
**RULES OF THE GAME**

*Aim of the Game*: To checkmate the opponent's king with any chess pieces on a 8×8 grid.

*Number of Players*: Two

*Materials Needed*: King, queen, two rooks, two bishops, two knights, and eight pawns for Red and for Blue; 8×8 grid.

*Preparation*: The chess pieces are set up as shown.

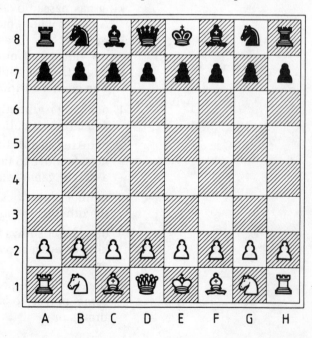

*How to Play*: This is the standard game of chess. You already know the basic moves of the chess pieces. Players alternate moves. Traditional chess sets have white and black chess pieces, and white moves first.

On its first move *only*, a pawn may go forward *one* or *two* squares. But if a pawn chooses to go forward two squares when it could have been captured immediately by the opponent's pawn if it had only gone one square, the opponent *on the next move only* may capture it as if it had moved only one square.

A pawn that reaches the far end of the grid (row 1 or 8) is *promoted*; the player chooses a queen, rook, bishop, or knight to replace it.

Under certain conditions each player may move both king and rook *at the same time* once during a game. This is *castling*. The conditions are:

1. neither the king nor rook has moved yet,

2. the squares between them are empty, and

3. the square the king is in, the square the king will cross, and the square the king will land in cannot be reached by the opponent in one move.

If these conditions are met, the king moves two squares toward the rook, and the rook moves to the square the king has passed over.

A player whose move directly attacks the opponent's king—that is, threatens to capture it on the next move—must call out "check." The other player must then get the king out of attack on the next move.

The game continues until:

1. one king is directly attacked and has no safe move to make (this is called *checkmate*), or

2. one king is *not* directly attacked and on its turn has no safe move to make (this is called *stalemate* and is a drawn game—no winner), or

3. neither player has sufficient forces left to checkmate the other (this too is a drawn game), or

4. one player shows he or she can check the opponent's king on *every* move (that player may declare a draw), or

5. the exact same position occurs three times, with the same player to move (that player may declare a draw), or

6. no pawn has been moved or piece captured for fifty consecutive moves (either player may declare a draw).

## PAWNS VERSUS PAWNS

We begin with a simple game, using just one kind of chess piece, the pawn, and a small grid.

### SC 20–1 (LL)
#### RULES OF THE GAME

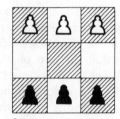

Starting position

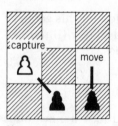

How pawn captures and moves

*Aim of the Game*: To be first to move one of your pawns to the opposite end of the board, or to capture or block all your opponent's pawns from moving.

*Number of Players*: Two

*Materials needed*: Three red and three blue pawns; 3×3 grid.

*Preparation*: The chess pieces are set up as shown.

*How to Play*: Players alternate turns. On each turn a pawn may either:

1. move one square straight forward to an empty square, red pawns toward row 3 and blue pawns toward row 1, or

2. move diagonally forward to an adjacent square occupied by an opposing pawn, remove it from the grid, and occupy the square it was in.

The first player to move a pawn all the way to the opposite end of the board, or to capture or block all the opponent's pawns from moving, wins.

### SC 20–2 (LL)
Same as SC 20–1, but with four pawns on each side in rows 1 and 4 of a 4×4 grid, instead of three pawns on each side of a 3×3 grid.

### SC 20–3 (LL)
Same as SC 20–1, but with five pawns on each side in rows 1 and 5 of a 5×5 grid, instead of three pawns on each side of a 3×3 grid.

Here's how a game of SC 20–1 might go:

```
B B B    B B B    B – B    B – B    B – –
– – –    R – –    B – –    R – –    R – B
R R R    – R R    – R R    – – R    – – R
```

Red is blocked, Blue wins.

Here's another example of a game:

```
B B B    B B B    B B –    B B –    – B –    R B –
– – –    R – –    R – B    R R B    R B B    – B B
R R R    – R R    – R R    – – R    – – R    – – R
```

Red's pawn has reached the opposite end of the grid. Red wins.

There are really not many different moves that can be made in this game. Play enough times so that you are completely familiar with the winning strategy. . . .

```
B B B
R – –
– R R
```

Have you recognized that the two positions on the left are really the same? They are symmetrical to each other. Go back to page 91 if you don't remember what that means. Since these positions are symmetrical, if

```
B B B
– – R
R R –
```

you figure out the strategy for one, you can apply it to the other too.

The general conclusion for this game is: By using the best moves, the second player (Blue) can always win, no matter what Red does.

## KNIGHTS CHANGE PLACES

The next game introduces a new chess piece, the knight, and makes you familiar with how the knight moves.

## SC 21–1 (LL)

### RULES OF THE GAME

*Aim of the Game:* To have the four red knights change places with the four blue knights by moving as the knight does in chess.

*Number of Players:* One or two.

*Materials Needed:* Four red and four blue knights; 5×5 grid.

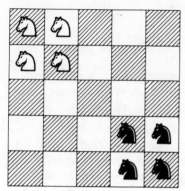

Starting position

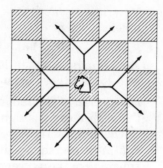

How knights move

*Preparation*: The knights are arranged on the grid as shown.

*How to Play*: The red and blue knights alternate turns. With two players, one player controls each color. On each move a knight moves to the next square up, down, left, or right (which need not be empty), then continues one square diagonally away from the starting square. The knight ends each move on an empty square of a different color from its starting square.

With one player, the game ends when the eight knights have changed places. *Any* red knight may end up in A4, A5, B4, or B5, and *any* blue knight may end up in D1, D2, E1, or E2. The player tries to accomplish this in as few moves as possible.

With two players, the player wins whose knights first occupy the squares from which the four knights of the other color started.

Notice that this game is similar in form to SM 8–2a (four cards change places, corner to corner), but how the cards move is different in each game.

**PIECES CAPTURE TOKENS**

## SC 22–1 (LL)
### RULES OF THE GAME

*Aim of the Game*: To capture as many tokens as possible by moves of your knight.

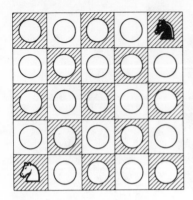

Starting position

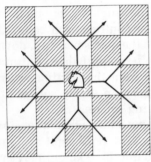

How knight moves

*Number of Players:* Two

*Materials Needed:* One blue knight, one red knight; 23 tokens; 5×5 grid.

*Preparation:* The knights are set up in diagonally opposite corners. A token is placed on every square of the grid except those occupied by the knights.

*How to Play:* The red and blue knights alternate turns. On each move a knight moves to the next square up, down, left, or right (which need not be empty), then continues one square diagonally away from the starting square. The knight ends each move on a square of a different color from its starting square.

A knight that lands on a square with a token in it captures and removes that token. A knight may not move into a square where it can be captured by the other knight.

The game ends when all tokens have been captured. The player who has taken more tokens wins.

### SC 22–2 (LL)

Same as SC 22–1, but with 47 tokens on a 7×7 grid, instead of 23 tokens on a 5×5 grid. This game can also be played by three or four players, each using a different face-up playing card as a knight, and each starting in a different corner.

### SC 22–3 (LL)

Same as SC 22–1, but with two *rooks* instead of two knights.

### SC 22–4 (LL)

Same as SC 22–1, but with two *rooks* instead of two knights, and 47 tokens on a 7×7 grid, instead of 23 tokens on a 5×5 grid.

---

## PAWNS VERSUS VARIOUS PIECES

---

### SC 23–1 (ML)
**RULES OF THE GAME**

*Aim of the Game:* For Blue, to move a pawn to row 1 without being captured there. For Red, to have knights capture all Blue's pawns or block them from moving on a 5×5 grid.

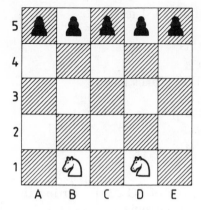

Starting position

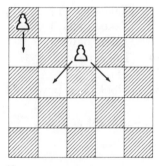

How pawns move

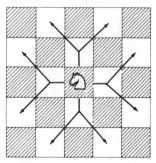

How knight moves

*Number of Players*: Two

*Materials Needed*: Five blue pawns and two red knights; 5×5 grid.

*Preparation*: The chess pieces are set up as shown.

*How to Play*: One player controls the blue pawns, the other player the red knights. Players alternate moves.

Pawn moves first. On each turn a pawn may either:

1. move one square straight forward to an empty square toward row 1, *or*

2. move diagonally forward to an adjacent square occupied by an opposing knight, remove it from the grid, and occupy the square it was in.

On each move a knight moves to the next square up, down, left, or right (which need not be empty), then continues one square diagonally away from the starting square. The knight ends each move on a square of a different color from its starting square. A knight captures and removes any pawn whose square it lands in. A knight may not land on a square that the other knight occupies.

The game ends when Blue gets a pawn to row 1 without its being immediately captured there, or when Red captures or blocks from moving all of Blue's pawns.

## SC 23–2 (ML)

Same as SC 23–1, but with two bishops starting at B1 and C1, instead of two knights at B1 and D1. On each turn a bishop moves on a diagonal line as many squares as desired, forward or backward. A bishop meeting a pawn captures it, removes it from the grid, and occupies the square it was in.

## SC 23–3 (ML)

Same as SC 23–1, but with a queen starting at C1, instead of two knights at B1 and D1. On each turn the queen moves horizontally, vertically, or diagonally as many squares as desired, in any direction, unless obstructed by a pawn. Upon meeting a pawn, the queen captures it, removes it from the grid, and occupies the square it was in.

Here's how a game of SC 23–1 might go:

| Pawns | Knights | |
|-------|---------|---|
| C5–C4 | B1–C3 | |
| B5–B4 | C3–D5 | (Takes pawn.) |
| C4–C3 | D1–E3 | |
| E5–E4 | E3–C2 | |
| B4–B3 | C2–A3 | |
| C3–C2 | D5–E3 | |
| C2–C1 | (Wins.) | |

And here's another game of SC 23–1, starting the same way, with a different outcome:

| Pawns | | Knights | |
|-------|---|---------|---|
| C5–C4 | | B1–C3 | |
| B5–B4 | | C3–D5 | (Takes pawn.) |
| C4–C3 | | D5–C3 | (Takes pawn.) |
| B4–C3 | (Takes kt.) | D1–C3 | (Takes pawn.) |
| E5–E4 | | C3–E4 | (Takes pawn.) |
| A5–A4 | | E4–C3 | |
| A4–A3 | | C3–B2 | (Blocks last pawn, wins.) |

Here's how a game of SC 23–2 might go:

| Pawns | Bishops | |
|-------|---------|---|
| B5–B4 | C1–B2 | |
| E5–E4 | B1–C2 | |
| C5–C4 | C2–A4 | |
| B4–B3 | B2–C3 | |
| E4–E3 | C3–A5 | (Takes pawn.) |
| E3–E2 | A5–E1 | |
| B3–B2 | A4–C2 | |
| C4–C3 | C2–B1 | |
| D5–D4 | B1–C2 | |
| D4–D3 | C2–D3 | (Takes pawn.) |
| C3–C2 | D3–C2 | (Takes pawn.) |
| B2–B1 | C2–B1 | (Takes pawn, wins.) |

Here's how a game of SC 23–3 might go:

| Pawns | Queen | |
|-------|-------|---|
| C5–C4 | C1–B2 | |
| E5–E4 | B2–B5 | (Takes pawn.) |

| Pawns | Queen | |
|-------|-------|---|
| E4–E3 | B5–B4 | (Takes pawn.) |
| D5–D4 | A5–B4 | |
| E3–E2 | B4–E1 | |
| D4–D3 | E1–C1 | |
| E2–E1 | C1–E1 | (Takes pawn.) |
| C4–C3 | E1–C3 | (Takes pawn.) |
| D3–D2 | C3–D2 | (Takes pawn, wins.) |

Sometimes it's hard to see a clear difference between strategy, or your general plans for reaching a goal, and tactics, or your more specific ways to carry out those plans. In the game of chess, this difference is often clearer than usual. In the two sample games of SC 23–1, you can see certain kinds of tactics used. For example, the knight's first move to C3 allows it to threaten the two pawns at B5 and D5. Only one can be moved to safety, and the knight can then capture the other. This tactic is similar to getting three in a row open at both ends in the game SM 15–1, where the goal was to get four in a row. The opponent can close only one end, and you can place your fourth card at the other end. Correspondingly, the pawns used a *tactic* of setting up formations where they protected each other. For example, in each game a chain A5, B4, C3 was set up, where the pawn at A5 protected the pawn at B4, which in turn protected the pawn at C3.

In the second game, the knights used a strategy of controlling the center. Looking back at the record of that game, you will see that four of the seven knights' moves were to C3, the central square. The knights won that game. By contrast, in the first game, which the knights lost, only one of six moves was to the central square.

This is not a coincidence. In chess, as in many other board games of strategy, control of the center is very important, basically because placing your pieces in the center gives you the greatest possible freedom of action. In this game, the knights can move quickly from the center to attack the pawns on row 5, and they can also move quickly to defend against a pawn reaching the first row. From the central square, C3, a knight can reach eight different squares on one move, more than from any other position.

Play SC 23–1 many times, taking sometimes the pawns and sometimes the knights. Then try SC 23–2 and SC 23–3. See what strategies and tactics you can develop. . . .

### PAWNS VERSUS KINGS

## SC 24–1 (ML)
### RULES OF THE GAME

*Aim of the Game*: For Blue, to move a pawn to row 1 without being captured there or to checkmate the king. For Red, to have the king capture all blue's pawns or block them from moving.

*Number of Players*: Two

*Materials Needed*: Five blue pawns and red king; 5×5 grid.

*Preparation*: The chess pieces are set up as shown.

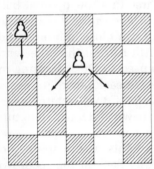

How pawns move

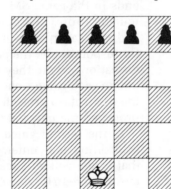

Starting position

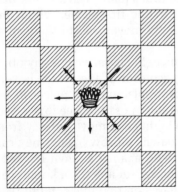

How king moves

*How to Play*: One player controls the blue pawns, the other player the king. Players alternate moves.

Pawns move first. On each turn a pawn moves one square straight forward to an empty square toward row 1.

On each turn the king moves one square horizontally, vertically, or diagonally in any direction, but it may *not* move into a square where it can be captured. Upon meeting a pawn, the king captures it, removes it from the grid, and occupies the square it was in.

The game ends when Blue gets a pawn to row 1 without its being immediately captured there, or a pawn checkmates the king, or when Red captures or blocks from moving all of Blue's pawns.

Here's how a game might go:

| Pawns | | King | |
|-------|--|------|--|
| C5–C4 | | C1–C2 | |
| D5–D4 | | C2–B2 | |
| B5–B4 | | B2–C2 | |
| B4–B3 | | C2–B2 | |
| D4–D3 | | B2–C3 | |
| D3–D2 | | C3–D2 | (Takes pawn.) |
| B3–B2 | | D2–C2 | |
| C4–C3 | | C2–C3 | (Takes pawn.) |
| B2–B1 | (Wins.) | | |

## KING VERSUS VARIOUS PIECES

### SC 25–1 (HL)
**RULES OF THE GAME**

*Aim of the Game*: For Blue, to checkmate the king with king, queen, and rook. For Red, to produce a drawn game.

*Number of Players*: Two

*Materials Needed*: Blue king, queen, and rook, red king; 5×5 grid.

*Preparation*: The chess pieces are set up as shown.

*How to Play*: Player alternates moves, with Blue going first. Blue may move the blue king, queen, or rook. The king moves one square horizontally, vertically, or diagonally in any direction, but it may *not* move into a square where it can be captured. The queen moves horizontally, vertically, or diagonally as many squares as desired, in any direction. A rook moves horizontally or vertically as many squares as desired. A king, queen, or rook landing in a square occupied by an opponent's chess piece captures and removes it. No chess piece may land in or pass over a square occupied by another piece of the same color.

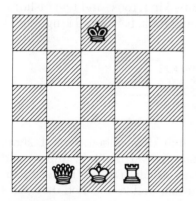

Starting position

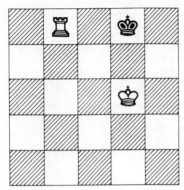

Example of checkmate,
Black's move

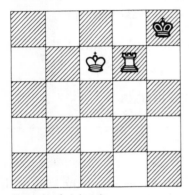

Example of stalemate,
Black's move

A player whose move directly attacks the opponent's king—that is, threatens to capture it on the next move—must call out "check." The other player must then get the king out of attack on the next move.

The game continues until:

1. one king is directly attacked and has no safe move to make (this is called *checkmate*), or

2. one king is *not* directly attacked and on its turn has no safe move to make (this is called *stalemate* and is a drawn game—no winner), or

3. neither player has sufficient forces left to checkmate the other (this too is a drawn game).

### SC 25–2 (HL)

Same as SC 25–1, but Blue king and two rooks, instead of king, queen, and rook, battle Red King. Row 1 set-up as shown.

### SC 25–3 (HL)

Same as SC 25–1, but Blue king, rook, and two knights, instead of king, queen, and rook, battle Red king. Row 1 set-up as shown.

### SC 25–4 (HL)

Same as SC 25–1, but Blue king, rook, and two bishops, instead of king, queen, and rook, battle Red king. Row 1 set-up as shown.

### SC 25–5 (HL)

Same as SC 25–1, but Blue king, queen, rook, bishop, knight, and five pawns, instead of king, queen, and rook, battle the same Red pieces. This is the set-up for each player: Blue on rows 1 and 2, and Red on rows 4 and 5. The aim of each player is to checkmate the other.

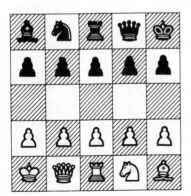

Starting position

Here's how a game of SC 25–2 might go:

| Blue | Red | |
|------|-----|---|
| B1–B3 | C5–C4 | |
| D1–D3 | C4–C5 | (Only move possible.) |
| B3–C3 | C5–B4 | |
| C1–C2 | B4–B5 | |
| D3–D4 | B5–A5 | (Only move possible.) |
| C3–C5 | | |
| (Checkmate.) | | |

Here's how a game of SC 25–3 might go:

| Blue | Red | |
|------|-----|---|
| D1–D3 | C5–C4 | |
| C1–C2 | C4–B4 | |
| D3–C3 | B4–A4 | |
| B1–A3 | A4–B4 | |
| C3–B3 | A4–A5 | (Only move possible.) |
| A3–C4 | A5–A4 | |
| C2–C3 | | |

Stalemate: Red has no safe move to make but is not directly attacked. The game is drawn.

Here's how a game of SC 25–5 might go:

| Blue | | Red | |
|------|---|-----|---|
| C2–C3 | | B4–C3 | (Takes pawn.) |
| D2–C2 | (Takes pawn.) | D4–C3 | (Takes pawn.) |
| E1–C3 | (Takes pawn, check.) | A5–C3 | (Takes bishop.) |
| D1–C3 | (Takes bishop.) | B5–C3 | (Takes knight.) |
| C1–C3 | (Takes knight.) | D5–D2 | |
| C3–C2 | | D2–B4 | |
| A2–A3 | | B4–A5 | |
| C2–C3 | | C5–D5 | |
| C3–C4 | (Takes pawn.) | A5–D2 | |
| B1–E4 | (Checkmate.) | | |

## PLACE AND MOVE

### SC 26–1 (HL)

#### RULES OF THE GAME

*Aim of the Game*: To choose places for chess pieces on board, and then checkmate the opponent's king.

*Number of Players*: Two

*Materials Needed*: King, queen, two rooks, two bishops, two knights, and eight pawns for Red and for Blue; 8×8 grid.

*How to Play*: Blue places any blue piece except the king on any empty square in rows 1 to 4; then Red places any red piece except the king in any empty square in rows 5 to 8. The players continue alternately placing their pieces on the board in the same way. The kings are the last to be placed, and they may not be placed where immediate capture is possible.

When all pieces have been placed, play begins according to the moves of the standard chess game. (see SC 19–1.

## APPLICATIONS

You have learned the moves of all the pieces, along with some basic chess strategy. You can now return to SC 19–1 and begin to play and enjoy the standard chess game played around the world. As you improve, you can turn to many other books dealing exclusively with chess strategy and tactics.

Over the course of several chapters, you have learned how to play a great many games and you have also learned some strategic principles to apply in these games. When you know a good strategy for a game, you play better. Some of these strategic principles apply beyond the games in which you learned them. Some apply to other games, as well as to real life situations, which makes them especially useful. Now we are going to give you practice in applying strategic principles from games to new situations. First, here's a list of some strategic principles you learned that apply beyond the games in which you learned them.

1. "Different" patterns may actually be the same.
2. Plan ahead.
3. Develop rules that eliminate possibilities.
4. Set up subgoals.
5. Work backwards from the goal.
6. Measure your distance from the goal, so you can plot your progress.
7. Watch your opponent's moves.
8. Get to the next subgoal the same way you got to the last.
9. Carry out a diversionary attack; then attack elsewhere.
10. Prepare your development; don't aim directly at the goal.
11. Make sure there is not an immediate threat of your losing.
12. Look for all possibilities.
13. Anticipate your opponent's moves.
14. Record your moves so you can learn from your experiences.

15. Recognize patterns; know what to do with a pattern you recognize.

16. If a good "move" doesn't work now, try it later.

17. You can obtain strategic principles through:
    a. logic,
    b. others' experience, and
    c. your own experience.

18. In some situations it's best to be on offense, others on defense.

19. It's best to choose a winning move, next best a move leading to a winning move, and next best again a move that avoids losing.

20. Have a strategy!

21. Know what the "aim of the game" is.

22. If the game isn't working, change the rules.

Let's apply some of these principles, beginning with Tony's problem.

---

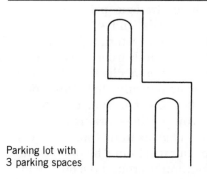

Parking lot with
3 parking spaces

Tony's parking lot holds three cars. The shape of his lot and how he arranges the cars in it are shown at the left. Tony has three regular customers:

1. A arrives at 8 AM and leaves at 4 PM.

2. B arrives at 9 AM and leaves at 6 PM.

3. C arrives at 10 AM and leaves at 5 PM.

Tony wants to avoid moving cars from one parking spot in his lot to another when he doesn't have to. Where should he have each customer park?

---

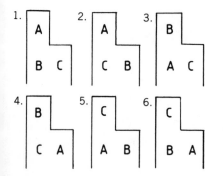

What strategic principles can help us here? Let's start with #12: Look for all possibilities. At the left are the possible ways to have the cars arranged on the lot between 10 AM and 4 PM.

Now let's look at strategic principle #3: Develop rules that eliminate possibilities. One principle would be that a car that always arrives later than the others should not be parked in the blocked spot. Another principle would be that a car that always leaves earlier than the others should not be parked in a blocked spot.

Arrangements 5 and 6 require a car to be moved to park C when it arrives at 10 AM. Arrangement 3 requires a car to be moved to park B when it arrives at 9 AM. Arrangements 1 and 2 require a car to be moved out of the way when car A leaves at 4 PM. Only arrangement 4 does not require moving a car from one spot to another. That is the arrangement Tony should use.

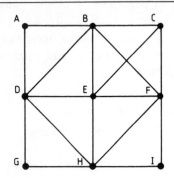

Enterprise Airlines has a special deal: for $200 you may fly anywhere in their network of cities (shown at the left) for two weeks, but you may only visit or pass through each city once. Each letter represents a city, and a line connects each pair of cities you can fly between. As a tourist, can you plan a route in which you start in E, visit all the cities, and return to E?

Here you can use three strategic principles—#2: Plan ahead, #4: Set up subgoals, and #5: Work backwards from the goal. You want to return to E at the end of your trip, but you can't get to E from A, G, or I. So your last subgoal must be a different city from A, G, or I. Try D as your last stop before returning to E. How could you have gotten to D? If you came from B, you will never have visited A. If you contine working backward from the goal, setting up subgoals in this way, you will see that you must begin your trip from E by first visiting either B, C, or F, and continuing around the outer edge.

# 5

# Games and Creativity

—What creative thinking is
—Creative thinking in games
—Creative thinking in real life
—A checklist for getting new ideas

## WHAT CREATIVE THINKING IS

If you have played the games in the previous chapters and followed our instructions about applications, you know that you have already experienced an increase in your deductive logic, inductive logic, and strategy muscles. But whether you know it or not, you have also increased your creative thinking ability. In this chapter, we will describe creative thinking, how you have already increased your creative thinking ability, and how you can continue to increase it both in playing games and in everyday life.

To put it simply and roughly, creative thinking means *coming up with new ideas*. An idea may still be new to *you*, although someone else somewhere else has already thought of it. As long as it's new to you, it qualifies as creative thinking. There are many ways to get new ideas, such as thinking of similar situations, forming analogies, using your imagination, and even, as we shall see, using a checklist.

Let's look at three different *uses* for creative thinking.

1. Sometimes you use creative thinking to come up with new alternatives when you are stuck in a situation.

> *Example*: After a long wait, you are finally seated at a table in the restaurant. Now you want to give your order, but the waiter ignores your calls each time he passes by. You need a new approach that works better.

You might:

- speak to the manager (like the time you spoke to the bank president because a teller was rude to you);
- walk over to the waiter and block his path so he can't ignore you;
- write your order on a slip of paper and bring it to the kitchen yourself (as you would serve yourself at a self-service gas station); or
- make a paper airplane from a $5 bill, and fly it at the waiter. (There's imagination at work, trying to get the waiter's attention!)

Can you think of other alternatives? We'll give you some more later in this chapter.

2. At other times, things are going well, but you use creative thinking to make them even better.

> *Example*: You wonder how you can encourage your children to read good books more often.

You might:

- begin reading an interesting book to them and then leave it around for them to finish;
- *forbid* them to read a book you want them to read;
- take them to an exciting movie based on a book you want them to read and then tell them "the book was even better"; or
- tell them that a book you want them to read was written by the same author as another book they have already read and enjoyed.

3. At still other times, you use creative thinking to figure out something that puzzles you.

> *Example*: You wonder why parking meters in Montreal are placed on the sidewalk near the buildings, instead of near the curb as in other North American cities.

> You think perhaps:

> - doing so made the city distinctive for *Expo '67*;
> - this was the result of a dispute between French-speaking and English-speaking residents; or
> - the piled-up winter snows would block meters from view if they were placed near the curb.

No matter *why* you use creative thinking for solving a problem, the basic steps are the same:

- Gather *information* about the problem situation.
- *Restate* the exact *problem* as clearly as you can.
- Come up with as many *different and new ideas* for solving the problem as you can, no matter how silly they may seem.
- *Choose* the idea that is best for your purposes.
- *Evaluate* how good your idea is.

Whether you realize it or not, you've already followed these steps! Back in "How to Use the Book," we suggested that after mastering a game you should *change the rules* to create new games. We suggested further that you see which changes make the game more fun and which changes don't. If you followed our suggestions, you've already gotten practice with some of the basic steps of creative thinking:

1. By mastering the game we presented, you've *gathered information*.
2. By thinking of different ways to change the rules, you've come up with *different* ideas (step 3). And if you thought of ways to change the rules that we didn't suggest, you've come up with *new* ideas.
3. By seeing which changes made the game more fun, you've *chosen the ideas* you thought best and evaluated them (steps 4 and 5).

If you haven't yet followed our suggestion, it's not too late! Creative thinking fits in with the games of this book in two other major ways:

1. You can be creative in actually *playing the games*.
2. You can be creative in *applying the principles from the games to your life*.

## CREATIVE THINKING IN GAMES

### Deduction

In game D 1–5, the players agree on a category, such as objects in the room, famous people in history, or geographical places. Player *A* writes down one secret object (or person or place) that fits the category, and *B* asks questions about it that can be answered by "yes" or "no." Your progress is steadiest when you ask a question that eliminates 50 percent of all the alternatives, no matter whether the answer is "yes" or "no." For example, if the category is a person, you could ask:

1. Is the person male?
2. Was the person born in an odd-numbered year?
3. Was the person born between January and June (half of all the months)?
4. Does the person's last name begin with a letter from A to M (half of all the letters of the alphabet)?

If the category is a *place*, you could ask whether it is in the Northern Hemisphere. In these cases you use *creative thinking* to come up with ideas for questions that must eliminate half of the possibilities.

### Induction

In game I 6–1, you had to find the *general* rule of regular change in rank and suit. In two examples of "special" rules, both suit and rank made a difference. Through creative thinking, you might have come up with other "special" rules. For example, we might consider all aces, 4s, 7s, and kings to be in one category ("straight numerals or letters"), all 6s, 8s, 9s, and queens in another category ("curved numerals or letters"), and all 2s, 3s, 5s, 10s and jacks to be in a third category ("mixed straights and curves"). Look at the markings 1, 2, 3, . . . 10, J, Q, K on the cards so you see what we mean. A special rule might then be: straight, curved, mixed (repeat).

Or we might consider that the suit markings for some cards, like the 6 of diamonds, are symmetrical from top to bottom, while the suit markings for other cards, like the 6 of hearts, are not. Look again at the deck to see what we mean. A special rule might then be: symmetrical, not symmetrical (repeat).

Perhaps, through creative thinking, you could come up with even more ideas for special rules in this inductive logic game.

You may also have used creative thinking in some of the Applications in that same chapter. In Application #6, you may have come up with many different ideas for what the objects that are attracted by magnets have in common.

Can you think where else in the games of the previous chapters you may have already used *creative thinking*? . . .

### Strategy

In SM 17–1, where you tried to get three or more cards in a row, you learned that making two different threats at the same time would lead to getting three in a row, because your opponent could respond to only one of them on the next turn. Here is the basic situation for making two threats at the same time. The solid white cards are yours, the dashed-line card shows your move that creates the situation.

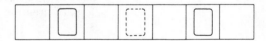

Through creative thinking you might have come up with many other situations where you could make two threats at the same time to get three in a row. Here are some of them (the black cards are your opponent's.):

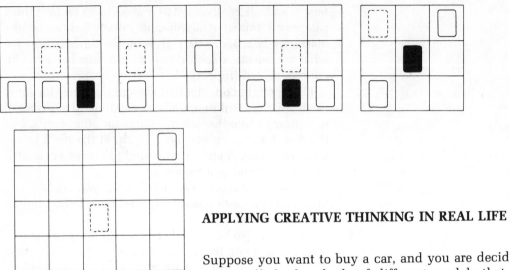

## APPLYING CREATIVE THINKING IN REAL LIFE

Suppose you want to buy a car, and you are deciding among all the hundreds of different models that are available. It's a confusing situation. You might apply some of your thinking muscles in these ways:

1. *Induction*: What generalizations can I make about the *kinds* of cars with which my friends have been happy and unhappy? My friends have been happy with Japanese cars made since 1974, happy with front-wheel drive cars, and unhappy with eight-cylinder engine cars, and so on.
2. *Strategy*: As I plan ahead, will I need a station wagon next year when my family is bigger? How well will different cars keep their resale value in the future?

Now let's see how you could apply the five basic steps of creative thinking.

### Step 1: Gathering Information.
By using induction and strategy, you have already taken the first step of gathering information. You have some idea of what you need and what to get.

### Step 2: Restating the Problem
What exactly is the problem? Originally, you have stated it as, "I need to buy a car and I don't know which

to get." But let's see what changes we can make in the "Aim of the Game" through creative thinking. Here are some possible alternative ways to state your problem:

1. I really need a form of transportation.
2. I just need a form of transportation for getting to work.
3. I really need a way to impress my friends with an expensive purchase.
4. I really need to protect myself against inflation.

Notice that the third alternative statement could lead to buying something else, and the fourth statement could lead to investing in the stock market! Suppose, however, you decide that your problem is really that you need a form of transportation for getting to work. You are now ready for the third step.

### Step 3: Many New and Different Ideas
Here are some alternatives you might come up with:

1. Move close to work so I can walk.
2. Change jobs.
3. Use my bicycle instead of a car.
4. Take taxis.
5. Stop working.
6. Work at home.
7. Buy a car.
8. Rent a car.
9. Buy a car to share with others.
10. Build my own car.
11. Use a car for transportation and to live in too.
12. Use a car for business and personal needs.
13. Have my company buy a car for me.

Some of these alternative are ways to get to work (such as by bicycle and by taxi), and others (such as stop working) change the statement of the problem once again, and bring you back to step 2. Often in creative thinking we move forward from one step to the next and then jump back again. This is nothing to worry about. Once your creative thinking starts flow-ing, you can't predict where it will take you. If you could, it wouldn't be very creative, would it?

### Step 4: Choose the Best Idea

At some point, when you are satisfied with how you have stated the problem and with the number of ideas you have, you begin to choose among these ideas. We say "begin" because the insights you get in making your choices might lead you back to an earlier step. For example, to seriously consider using your bicycle in-stead of a car, you may have to find out how long the trip from home to work by bicycle would take (gather more information).

To choose among your ideas, you first need to think of the advantages and disadvantages of each. For example, taking your bicycle to work may be cheaper and give you needed exercise (advantages), but doing so may take too long, tire you out, not allow you to shop after work and bring home packages, and be dangerous during rush hours (disadvantages). You then look at how important these advantages and disadvantages are to you. For example, the money you save taking your bicycle might be important enough to you to outweigh all the disadvantages. Or the possible danger from bicycle riding might outweigh all the advantages.

### Step 5: Evaluate Your Idea

Once you feel one idea is clearly the best, your next step is to evaluate it. This usually means trying it out and seeing how well it works. Again, there are *alternate* ways to evaluate your idea.

1. You could more thoroughly trace in your mind all the steps involved in carrying out your idea and all the effects of the idea. For example, if you rode your bicycle to work, where would you keep it? Perhaps there is no good place to keep it—a new disadvan-tage. Maybe you don't need to have your own bicycle because before and after work you could borrow the bicycle from the company messenger—a new advan-tage.

2. You could talk to people who already are using your idea and see what they think of it. For example, if

you know people who ride their bicycles to work, you could talk to them about it. If you don't, you could stop someone you don't know who is riding to work. Chances are the person will enjoy being asked for his or her opinion.

3. You could *observe* people who are already using your idea, thereby getting new information to help you evaluate your idea. For example, you notice that someone riding a bicycle to work gets splashed by a passing car. Now you know a disadvantage you hadn't thought of.

### Applying the Steps

Let's see how to apply creative thinking to the simpler, everyday situation mentioned earlier. After a long wait, you are finally seated at a table in the restaurant. Now you want to give your order, but the waiter ignores your calls each time he passes by. You need a new approach that works better.

As we apply the five basic steps of creative thinking to this situation, notice once again how the other skills, such as induction, also play a role.

1. Gather information about the problem situation.

a. *Induction:* Is he ignoring all his customers? Only those who are not dressed well? Only the loud parties? Are the other waiters also giving poor service?

2. Restate the exact problem as clearly as you can. Some possibilities are:

a. He doesn't like me.

b. The restaurant is crowded and understaffed today.

c. I haven't really been waiting that long, but I skipped breakfast and am very hungry so it seems like poor service.

d. The problem may be in the kitchen (leading to gather more information—are other people getting their food?)

3. Come up with as many different ideas for solving the problem as you can, no matter how silly they may seem. At this point stop reading and list as many different ideas as fast as you can for dealing with the situation. Don't worry now about how practical the ideas

are. When you slow down, look back at the first two steps (gather information and restate the problem) for inspiration. Look also at the ideas you already have: Do they suggest others to you? When you feel *all* your ideas have been written down, compare them with the following list. Are there some that you have and we don't? Are there some that we have and you don't? Start making your list now. . . .

a. Speak to the manager.

b. Walk over to the waiter; block his path so he can't ignore you.

c. Drop a plate.

d. Move to a table the waiter must pass more frequently in going into and out of the kitchen (strategy—making general plans to reach your goal).

e. Speak more loudly the next time the waiter comes by.

f. Go to a different restaurant.

g. Write your order on a slip of paper and bring it to the kitchen yourself.

h. Offer to help the waiter with some of his other tables.

i. Make a paper airplane from a $5 bill, and fly it at the waiter.

j. Offer to buy the waiter roller skates.

k. Join a friend at another table who's already been served.

l. Startle the waiter by asking for your check!

m. Take off your clothing to attract the waiter's attention.

n. Pretend to be choking.

o. Offer to buy food from someone at another table who's getting good service.

p. Read a newspaper or work on something else to pass the time while you wait.

q. Start to walk out; when you are stopped, tell the cashier your problem.

r. Call a pizza parlor and have them deliver pizza to your table.

s. Rattle silverware against your glass.

t. Faint.

4. Choose the idea best for your purposes. Your choice will depend on what information you have gathered, how you've stated the problem, what ideas you've come up with, what advantages and disadvantages you see in these ideas, and, of course, what you are like as a person.

5. Evaluate how good your idea is. Suppose you have decided that your best idea after all is to go to a different restaurant. You will surely notice how long it takes to be waited on at that second restaurant. And if you care enough, before you leave the first restaurant, you might ask a friend who has just entered to sit at the table you are leaving and to call you that evening and let you know how long it took to get waited on.

## TOOLS FOR CREATIVE THINKING

To help you carry out all five steps in creative thinking, here are:

- a *worksheet* to record your progress on a problem,
- a general *checklist* for getting ideas for all solving all kinds of problems,
- an *example* of how the worksheet and checklist could be applied to the restaurant situation we have just been discussing. (Figs 5–1, 5–2, 5–3, and 5–4.)

When you use the checklist, try not only to think of new ideas for each item on it, but also to combine two different items on the checklist to get a new idea. For example, by combining "change flavor" and "substitute something else" in the restaurant situation, you might get the idea to eat the flowers on your table instead of ordinary food.

You have seen how the checklist can be applied to the restaurant problem, which is really a personal/social situation. Can you think of other situations very similar to it? Here's one:

You are a student in a class, and no matter how often you raise your hand, the teacher doesn't call on you.

**Figure 5–1**. *Worksheet to Record Your Five Steps in Creative Thinking*

The Problem: _____

1. Information
   gathered: _____
   _____
   _____
   _____
   _____
   _____

2. Problem
   restated: _____
   _____

3. *New Ideas:*                    *Advantages*          *Disadvantages*

4. Choice of
   best idea _____

5. Evaluation
   plan and
   results: _____

**Figure 5–2.** Worksheet to Record Your Five Steps in Creative Thinking

The Problem: How to get the waiter to stop ignoring me

1. Information gathered:
Service to everyone seems slow
Seems to be too few waiters for too many customers
Person at next table says she's been waiting 20 minutes

2. Problem restated: Even if I get waiter's attention, will I have to wait long for my food? Real problem is, "How can I get fed quickly?"

3. New Ideas:

| | Advantages | Disadvantages |
|---|---|---|
| Drop a plate | Will get attention | May have to pay for it |
| Speak to manager | Manager can direct waiter to serve me promptly. | I'll lose time finding and speaking to the manager. With too few waiters, management may not be able to help me. |
| Go to a different restaurant | Get away from unpleasant situation. Service will probably be better. | Takes time Service may not be better. |

4. Choice of best idea: Go to a different restaurant

5. Evaluation plan and results:
See how long it takes to be served in a different restaurant
Compare with service to friend who stayed at first restaurant

**Figure 5–3.** *Checklist for Getting New Ideas.*

Change
- meaning
- color
- motion
- texture
- form
- shape
- weight
- flavor
- sound
- use
- inside
- outside
- symmetry
- quality
- _____

Make bigger
- more time
- more often
- stronger
- some parts larger
- thicker
- add value
- add ingredient
- multiply
- exaggerate
- add parts
- blend
- make assortment
- add ideas
- add functions
- add purposes
- _____

Make smaller
- break up
- condense
- miniaturize
- lower
- shorten
- lighten
- omit something
- simplify
- thin out
- understate
- take parts away
- _____

Substitute something
- someone else
- something else
- somewhere else
- another material
- another process
- another source of power
- another approach
- another emotion
- another function
- another role
- _____
- _____

Rearrange
- more pieces
- different pattern
- different sequence
- reverse cause and effect
- change schedule
- reverse positive and negative
- opposites
- backward
- upside down
- _____
- _____

Use something similar
- another event
- another idea
- new ways to use
- something to copy
- _____
- _____

**Figure 5–4.** *Checklist for Getting New Ideas*
(Example of How to Use)

| | |
|---|---|
| Change | |
|     motion | Roller skates for waiter |
| Make bigger | |
|     more time | Read newspaper; be patient |
|     more often | Move to table he passes often |
|     stronger | Speak louder |
|     exaggerate | Choke; faint |
|     blend | Join friend at another table |
|     make assortment | Take small tastes of many other diners' meals |
|     add purposes | Offer to help waiter with other tables |
| Make smaller | |
|     omit something | Skip a meal |
|     simplify | Make your order simple: "Number seven, please" |
|     understate | Ask for check |
| Substitute something | |
|     something else | Candy bar from pocket |
|     somewhere else | Go to another restaurant |
|     another source of power | Speak to manager |
|     another emotion | Plead; yell |
| Rearrange | |
|     reverse cause and effect | Instead of "I've waited a long time so I'm hungry," think "I'm hungry so it feels like I've waited a long time." |
|     change schedule | Cancel later appointments; enjoy leisurely meal |
|     reverse positive and negative | Think "It's nice not being rushed in and out." |
|     backward | Ask for check |
| Use something similar | |
|     new ways to use | Use table as place for food from outside; order pizza |
|     something to copy | Pretend to be a waiter; pick up food from kitchen, bring it back to your table |

You can use the checklist here too; in fact, some of the same ideas for the restaurant situation might work here or lead to others that might work.

Here's another personal/social situation:

> You have been waiting one half-hour for your friend with whom you have an appointment. What might have happened? What should you do now?

Now let's look at how you could use the checklist for inspiration when you are faced with a physical problem.

> You return home and discover you don't have your front-door key with you, and the door is locked.

Write down as many alternatives as you can think of quickly for getting into your house. Then go through the checklist for further inspiration, and come up with as many more ideas as you can.

You have seen the five basic steps in creative thinking, how to use creative thinking in games, and how it applies to real-life problems. You have also had special help with the third step, coming up with many new and different ideas. Now it's up to you to exercise your creative thinking muscle.

# 6

# How to Benefit the Most from This Book

—Your attitude toward playing
—Discussion and playing
—Creating your own game variations
—Applying game principles in your own life
—Tips for parents and teachers

This book, as you have seen, can provide hours of fun. But you can also use the book to strengthen your muscles of the mind. If *that* is your purpose, this chapter shows you how to derive the most benefit from the book. If you are a parent or teacher who wants your children to derive the most educational benefit from the book, this entire chapter is essential reading. In addition, the final section on Special Tips for Parents and Teachers is written especially for you.

The first point to remember is that, just as you would work out regularly to build up your body muscles, you should set aside regular times to play games to increase your thinking skills. A daily session is best if you have the time; otherwise three times a week is adequate to involve you in games. When you play the games in this book regularly, you actively exercise your thinking skills. You actually learn many different things at the same time. At one level, you learn how to play the games well. It's always a good feeling, of course, to learn to do anything well. And as you play a game, you are exercising a major muscle of your mind, such as deductive logic or inductive logic. As you play many games from different chapters you are also developing habits of organized thinking, as well as learning to take systematic approaches to solving problems, to plan ahead, and to set priorities. Finally, you are also learning some personal and social skills such as cooperation, communication, dealing with others whose goals are incompatible with yours, and sensitivity to others—all skills that are vital both in playing games and in everyday life.

Because games contain all the basic elements of our everyday activities, everything you learn from games can be applied elsewhere in your life *if you work at doing so*. In this chapter, we show you *how* to transfer skills acquired in game-playing to your daily life. But we first must talk about:

1. your attitude toward playing,
2. how discussion helps learning, and
3. how to create your own game variations.


## YOUR ATTITUDE TOWARD PLAYING

Keeping a relaxed attitude toward the games you play is important. To do so, remember that a game is a safe situation in which to try out ways of thinking and strategies, not a duel to the death. When the emotional overtones of a game threaten its enjoyment or educational value, feel free to change the rules and get things back into perspective.

For example, two boys of different ages were playing ping-pong. The older boy, a much better player, won game after game. The younger boy was becoming more and more discouraged, and he was ready to quit. Even the older boy was not enjoying winning due to the big difference in their abilities. Suddenly the older boy suggested, "Instead of trying to beat the other guy, let's see how many times we can hit the ball back and forth to each other without being out." The younger boy found this new arrangement to be much more fun, and to the surprise of both found his ability improving too.

Even though you are competing with others, you

must cooperate to make a game a joyful experience for all the players. By cooperating, all the player can learn more, as well as have more fun. A friendly spirit among the players is important for the success of the next activity.

## DISCUSSION AND PLAYING

After you play a game, discuss it with the other players. You might need to write down all your actions and the reasons behind them in some games, so you can remember and discuss them later. Don't do this every time you play, of course, or you will lose the fun value of the game.

Then go over the game again, and, as you go over it, discuss it. Find out how each player made his or her decisions, talking about what else might have been done. You can learn from both "good" moves and mistakes. As you enter the minds of other people and see how they think, you can improve your own thinking and playing. When you play with weaker players, help them improve. By doing so, you'll be sharpening your understanding of the game too.

Here's a list of points to discuss for *any* game:

1. At each turn, why did you do what you did? For example, why did you put down that row of cards in D, guess that rule in I, move that card to there in S?
2. What are all the different reasons given for the players' actions?
3. Do they have different *general* approaches to the games?
4. What are the advantages and disadvantages of each approach?
5. Which approach works best?
6. Are there other approaches no one thought of during the game?

And here is a list of things to do *after* you discuss a game:

1. Play again, trying those approaches you decided were better. See how you've improved.

2. Play the same basic game at a higher level. Discuss it. Again, see how you've improved.

Finally, in choosing a game to play, consider these two points:

1. Practice more in a group of games where you are weak than in one where you are strong. If you have trouble with, for example, SM 12–1, stick with it.
2. Don't repeat a game over and over again if the same player always wins it. Switch games, or switch that player into a different group.

Now let's look at some more specific points for different kinds of games.

### Deductive Logic

Keep a careful record when you play the same game many times to see if you need fewer rows to figure out the code. Remember that in those games where you don't control which cards go into each row (such as D 3–1 and D 6–1) there is a large chance factor. Your records may show a general trend toward fewer rows needed, but the chance factor may produce bumps in this trend.

Remember one simple game you probably already know that makes use of deductive logic: 20 Questions. In this game, one player thinks of an object in the room, a geographic place, a person, or whatever the players agree on, and the other players ask questions that can be answered by "yes" or "no" to zero in on the object. When you play this game, it's important to devise questions that will group all possible objects (or places or persons) in a way that leads to efficient elimination. In game D 1–1, for example, it's advisable to begin with a question like, "Is it a black card?" Such a question eliminates 50 percent of the possibilities no matter what the answer is. Less advisable is a question like, "Is it a card with rank less than three?" This question might eliminate only 25 percent of the possibilities. Thus you attempt to divide all the possibilities into two equal groups, so that whether you get a "yes" or a "no," you can eliminate 50 percent of the possibilities. You then get the same amount of information regardless of the answer. But if your question divides all the possibilities up into groups of 90 percent and 10 percent, the answer might eliminate only 10 percent of the possibilities.

Correspondingly, in playing 20 Questions, begin with questions like, "Is the object on the left side of the room?" or "Is the object standing on the floor?" Avoid such questions as, "Is the object one with four legs made out of aluminum?" It's better to begin with, "Is this place in the Western Hemisphere?" than "Is it a river in Arkansas?" It's better to begin with "Is this person alive? . . . Is the person famous?" than with "Does the person work at the corner drugstore?"

When you discuss this game, you can learn which strategies other players have for efficient elimination. You may find that some players don't have *any* strategy! You can also discuss the strategy of the person who first thinks of the object, place, or person.

In playing D 2–1, to find the rank of two secret cards out of five, by choosing cards, which approaches to choosing cards worked? Were some codes easier to find out than others? Were some codes easier to fool the other players with? Were the tables in the Appendix helpful?

### Inductive Logic

You can use a number of principles in these games:

1. Try simple rules first.
2. Get more information.
3. List possibilities.
4. Eliminate possibilities.
5. Go back and forth between inductive and deductive logic.
6. The "same" event may have more than one meaning.
7. Pay attention to *all* changes from one "similar" event to another.
8. See what things that *don't* fit a rule have in common.
9. The same characteristics may make a difference in two different ways.
10. Look for a *cycle*, whch is a complete set of changes before a pattern repeats.

Is each player aware of these principles? Do two players using the same principle get the same result? For example, after the 3C, 9S, and 5H have been found that "fit the rule" in I 6, would every player list the same possibilities for what the rule is?

**Strategy**

In any *Strategy* game, the players alternate moves, choosing on each turn from among many possible moves. This gives you the opportunity to discuss such questions as:

1. In making this move, did you consider what the other player's response would be?

2. Were you concerned only about offense and not defense? For example, in SM 10–1, when you set up a chain to let your cards make multiple jumps, were you aware that the other player could also use the same chain? In SM 14–1, were you concentrating on getting your own three in a row, without paying attention to what the other player was doing?

3. How much did you plan ahead? In S 14–1, did you place your cards in good positions to move from later? In SC 13–1, did you place your cards in well thought-out relation to each other? In SC 16–1, how many moves ahead did you plan? Did you take into account what your opponent might do?

## CREATING YOUR OWN GAME VARIATIONS

Back in "How to Use the Book," we suggested that, after you master a game, you should change the rules to create your own game variations. Doing so allows you to enjoy many more different game activities while exercising the muscles of your mind, just as you might engage in many different activities (push-ups, chinning, weight-lifting) to exercise your arm muscles. Creating your own game variations also has the purpose, as we have seen in the last chapter, of improving your creative thinking.

Now let's go over together in some detail how you could change the rules of a game to create new games. First, here is a checklist of general features of any game you could look at to change.

1. the starting positions of the cards,
2. the size of the grid,
3. the number of players,
4. the number of cards,
5. the way the cards are moved,
6. the choices each player has,
7. ways of capturing,
8. the chance element,
9. how the game is scored,
10. what "winning" means, and
11. time limits.

You might even try a rule from one game in a completely different game.

Use this checklist with at least two different games in deductive logic, inductive logic, and strategy. Doing so gives you extra practice in all these skills plus creative thinking.

Let's now go over changing the rules of some games together. We'll begin with the rules for our very first Strategy game, S 1–1. For each statement in the rules, try to think of alternatives. In the following list, seven statements in the rules are accompanied by some alternatives we have thought of. There may, of course, be many others that we haven't given. The original rules are in regular type, and the alternatives are in italics:

1. *Aim of the Game*: To remove four out of five cards
   . . .
   *—to remove five out of six cards.*
   *— to remove six out of seven cards.*
   *— to remove four out of five cards and wind up with the fifth card on the edge of the grid.*
   *— to remove four out of five cards and wind up with the fifth card not on the edge of the grid.*

2. . . . by using a jump-and-take rule.
   *— by using a take-on-every-other-jump-rule.*
   *— by using a take-on-horizontal-jumps-only rule.*

3. *Preparation*: The cards are placed face down in the positions shown.

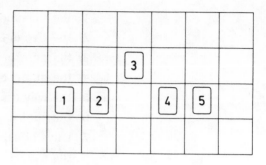

—in the positions shown.

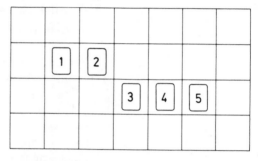

—in the positions shown below, where the black square cannot be crossed.

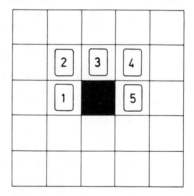

—in random positions on the grid.

4. For convenience, we label the cards from one to five.
   —we label the cards from one to five because they must be removed from the grid in that order.

5. Materials Needed: Five cards 4×7 grid.
   —six cards; 5×7 grid.
   —seven cards; 5×5 grid.
   —eight cards; 4×9 grid.

6. On each move the player picks one card to jump over another, horizontally or vertically . . .
   — *horizontally, vertically, or diagonally.*
   — *diagonally only.*
   — *a card can jump over two cards to an empty square just beyond.*
   — *a card can move or jump.*
   — *the player must alternate moves and jumps.*
7. The game continues until only one card remains.
   — *after every four moves, new cards are randomly added to the grid until the entire deck has been placed down.*

You've just seen some of the many ways the rules can be changed for a beginning strategy game. Now let's see how eight different statements in the rules can be changed for a more advanced Strategy game, SC 15–1.

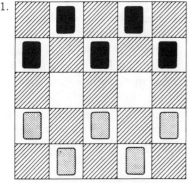

1. *Aim of the Game:* To capture all your opponent's cards by jumping diagonally or blocking them from moving.
   — *to block all your opponent's cards from moving.*
   — *to force your opponent to capture all your cards.*
   — *to capture all your opponent's cards by jumping horizontally or vertically.*
   — *to force your opponent to block all your cards from moving.*
2. *Number of Players:* Two
   — *three*
   — *four*
3. *Materials Needed:* Five red and five blue cards; 5×5 grid.
   — *eight red and eight blue cards; 8×8 grid.*
   — *eight red and four blue cards; 8×8 grid.*
4. *Preparation:* The cards are placed face down as shown in (1).
   — *the cards are placed face down as shown in 2.*
   — *the cards are placed down at random.*
5. On each turn a card either moves one square diagonally . . .
   — *moves one square horizontally or vertically . . .*

6. . . . or jumps diagonally over an opponent's card to an empty square just beyond, capturing and removing the opponent's card from the grid, and continuing to make more jumps on the same turn if possible.
   —*jumps diagonally on top of an opponent's card . . .*
   —*jumps diagonally over an opponent's card, which is then placed on any empty square of the player's choice . . .*

7. A player *must* capture at every opportunity but may choose which capture to make if there is more than one possibility.
   —*a player has the option of capturing or not capturing.*
   —*a player must capture at each opportunity, but the opponent chooses which card should be captured if there is more than one possibility.*

8. When a red card reaches row 1 or a blue card reaches row 5, it ends its turn, gets placed sideways, and is called a "king." A king moves and jumps like any other card, but in *any* diagonal direction.
   —*when a red card reaches row 1 or a blue card reaches row 5, it gets removed from the grid.*
   —*when a red card reaches row 1 or a blue card reaches row 5, it gets removed from the grid. The player may replace it on any empty square of the grid in his/her next move.*
   —*when a red card reaches row 1 or a blue card reaches row 5, the player may replace it immediately on any empty square of the grid.*

## APPLYING GAME PRINCIPLES IN YOUR OWN LIFE

After you have exercised and strengthened your muscles of the mind, the next step is to apply the principles you learn from the games to your everyday life. From games, you can learn how to form plans, eliminate possibilities, discover relationships, and other skills for transfer to solving problems in your daily life. But only you can do this; you can't depend on us. You must go beyond the book and work independently at transferring what you've learned to your everyday life.

To do so, read and work through the Applications section of a chapter after you play the games in it. Notice how game situations are related to other life situations. Your goal is to transfer what you have learned from the games to your life. When faced with a problem in your daily life, look for similar situations in the games and apply the principles you have learned. Let's now go over how you can do this with some of the major skills: deductive logic, inductive logic, and strategy.

### Deductive Logic

You have already seen in the Applications section how the principles you've learned from the card games can be applied to other situations. But unless you are a very unusual person, these other situations are not very real to you. Most of us in our daily lives do not have to figure out which customer shopped on which floor of a department store, or which coin in a group is counterfeit. So let's continue our step-by-step approach, and see how to apply the principles from the games to situations we are more likely to meet in our daily lives.

A common theme of *all* the games in the Deductive Logic chapter is how to eliminate possibilities in an organized, systematic way to reach an answer that must be so. Examples included a doctor isolating which of many possible factors is causing a rash, a driver narrowing down the reasons a car won't start, a person deciding which of many possible meals to serve dinner guests, and the police deciding which of many possible suspects has actually committed a crime. Can you think of other situations in your life where you have to systematically eliminate possibilities?

One situation that many of us face at one time or another is making a major purchase, such as a car, a house, or a television set. Many different cars, homes, or TV sets are available, and we need a way to systematically eliminate the possibilities to decide which to buy.

Let's say we want to buy a car. With hundreds of different makes and models of different years to consider, we face a complicated "one-out-of-many" situation. Here are some questions that we can ask ourselves to eliminate possibilities:

1. Do I want a new car or a used car?
2. How many people do I want it to seat?
3. How much luggage space do I need?
4. How much money am I willing to spend?
5. How important are safety features? Style considerations? Maintenance costs? Performance? Comfort?

If we can systematically answer these questions (and perhaps others) before we meet with a salesperson or look at advertisements, we are more likely to make a satisfying purchase.

Buying a gift for a friend is another complicated "one-out-of-many" situation. In fact, it can be even more complicated than the "major purchase" situation. Here are some questions you might begin by asking:

1. What do I think my friend would like to receive?
2. Do I want to choose a returnable gift in case I'm wrong?
3. What would *I* like to give that person?
4. How much money am I willing to spend?

If you decide that the person would like to receive a car, that you'd like to give one, and that you can afford to give one, then you've got to then answer all the questions related to buying a car!

Let's look now at another situation where you have to systematically eliminate possibilities. Your friend Sally was supposed to meet her Aunt Tilly at the airport, where she is arriving from out of town for a visit. But Sally, who isn't feeling well, has stayed home and asked you to meet her aunt. "You'll have no trouble recognizing her," Sally told you, "because she looks just like me." But you're at the airport now, and you *are* having trouble. Hundreds of people are leaving the jumbo-jet that has just arrived, and *none* of them looks like Sally. To make matters worse, the public address system is not working, so you can't have Sally's aunt paged.

You are in a one-out-of-many situation. Needing more information to eliminate possibilities, you step into a phone booth, from which you can still see the stream of passengers, and call Sally. You ask her such questions as:

1. How tall is she? (Just like, "Is the card a seven or higher?")
2. What color hair does she have? ("Is it a club or a spade?")
3. Is she heavy?
4. Does she wear glasses? And so on.

This information, plus the fact that Sally's aunt will be eagerly looking for Sally, should help you to reduce the possibilities.

In any situation—making a major purchase for yourself, buying a gift for someone else, meeting someone you don't know—the principles you've learned from the games in this chapter can be very helpful. We cannot guarantee you'll make the "right" decisions in a world that is much more complicated than any card game. But you can increase the chances that you'll make effective decisions.

### Inductive Logic

We want you to apply what you've learned about inductive logic to the complex situations of real life. Can you yourself think of situations in your life where you use, or could use, inductive logic to find rules? The following example may help you. A new person, Ted, comes to work in your company. He shares an office with you. Everyone, of course, wants to know what he's really like. Since you're in the best position to find out, they count on you to tell them. Here are some pieces of information you pick up, along with the possible rules you think of:

| *Information* | *Possible Rules* |
| --- | --- |
| He brings his lunch every day, never eats out with others. | He's saving money. |
| | He's cheap. |
| | He doesn't like people. |
| He doesn't say much in the office. | He's aloof. |
| | He's stupid. |

One day you happen to leave the building with Ted and walk with him to the bus stop, talking about a third person whom, it turns out, neither of you like. The next day Ted seems friendlier and starts conversations with you several times. You invite him to go out to lunch with you, and he accepts. You change your possible rules from, "He's saving money." to "He's shy, or he doesn't know anybody at work yet."

From the behaviors we notice in other people, we are constantly formulating "rules" about them. Often we are wrong, and, with new information and a willingness to change our minds, we correct our first impressions. For example, a salesperson's success depends on the ability to quickly form accurate rules about people. Certain rules help salespersons deal effectively with people they have just met moments ago. Here are some of them:

1. Which people are good prospects and which people are a waste of time?

2. What different categories of good prospects are there?

3. Which sales arguments work best with which category of prospect?

4. Which products is each category of prospect more likely to buy?

Sometimes one reaches a wrong conclusion because the "rule" is based on too few cases, or because one just comes across an exception.

Of course, people also form rules about particular family members and friends they have known for a long time:

1. what a person likes to do,

2. what a person doesn't want to hear about,

3. how to make a person happy, or

4. how to avoid making a person angry.

You are always using inductive logic to form rules about people you've just met and about people you've known a long time. You also use it to form rules about "people in general":

| | |
|---|---|
| 1. People are kind. | 3. People mean well. |
| 2. People can't be trusted. | 4. People are lazy. |

You also use inductive logic in such everyday activities as shopping:

1. This store has higher prices.
2. This brand means quality.
3. This brand just means you're paying more.

In all areas of your life, you have formed rules, often without being aware that you have done so. Every day you have opportunities to change these rules and to form new ones. By applying what you have learned about inductive logic, you can become a more effective and happier person.

### Strategy

In the Strategy games chapters, we applied strategic principles to problems with exact answers. Now let's look at some "messier" life situations, and see how strategic principles from the games you have learned can help. For example, you are beginning your freshman year at college. You do not know which courses to take. What should you do? Some of the strategic principles in the Applications section of the "Strategy Games of Conflict" chapter can help you in this situation:

1. Different patterns may actually be the same. Taking Economics the first semester and Anthropology the second semester may be the same to you as taking Anthropology the first semester and Economics the second semester.
3. Develop rules that eliminate possibilities. You can eliminate courses with prerequisites you haven't taken, along with courses you don't want and don't have to take.
4. Set up subgoals. If you want to take Psychology 301, for which Psychology 101 and Psychology 201 are prerequisites, begin by taking Psychology 101 now.
8. Get to the next subgoal the way you got to the last. Plan your second semester the same way you plan your first.

10. Prepare your development; don't aim directly at the goal. Take courses as a freshman that will help you later in college, such as English Composition. Select courses that you will need to take regardless of what you major in.

11. Make sure there is no immediate threat of your losing. If you are a weak student, unsure that you are "college material," begin by taking easy courses so you don't flunk out.

12. Look for all possibilities. Read the catalog.

16. If a good "move" doesn't work now, try it later. If a class you really want to take is filled up, check back in a week for vacancies.

17. You can obtain strategic principles through:
    a. Logic: Think through the situation. You can maintain flexibility by taking courses you will need to take no matter what you major in (see rule #10). Or you can use your freshman year to explore new fields you weren't exposed to in high school (such as Anthropology).
    b. Others' experience: Ask sophomore students for their opinions.
    c. Your own experience: Think of what your interests are, and what you enjoyed studying in high school.

21. Know the "aim of the game." Why are you going to college? To explore new fields, to meet a future husband or wife, to learn a profession, to get admitted to a professional school, to get a piece of paper that says you are a college graduate?

22. If the game isn't working, change the rules. If you are allowed to take five courses and you want to take six, ask the permission of the Dean. If you want to take a course and you don't have the prerequisites, ask the permission of the instructor to take it anyway.

In the last situation, you have a goal and face obstacles to reaching it, but no one is trying to prevent you from reaching the goal.

Now let's look at a case situation in which you must struggle against someone else. You are competing with co-workers in the same office for a promotion that has just opened up. What should your plan be? Here are some principles that might apply:

5. Work backwards from the goal. Tell the person who will make the promotion decision what you would do for the company if you got the promotion.

7. Watch your opponents' moves. If other workers are choosing to appear very busy as a way of winning the promotion, you can choose to be productive and stand out.

17. You can obtain strategic principles through:
    a. Logic: Which qualities are needed in the job? Make sure you show those qualities.
    b. Others' experience: What qualities have other workers in the firm had who got promoted?
    c. Your own experience: What qualities have others praised in you before?

18. In some situations it's better to be on offense, others on defense. Find out if the company is looking for a hard-driving aggressive person, or someone who can work smoothly with others.

19. It's best to choose a winning move, next best a move leading to a winning move, and next best again a move that avoids losing. Do what you can to get the promotion if it's possible. If it doesn't seem possible, learn something from the situation so you can get the next promotion that opens up. Finally, don't do anything that will get you fired!

20. Have a strategy! Here are some possible strategies: appear busy, be productive, demonstrate a unique skill.

Let's look next at another kind of struggle, where winning is more than just desirable, but rather necessary for survival. You are managing a political campaign, where you must receive at least 10 percent of the vote or your party will be abolished. How should you go about it? Here are some principles that may help:

6. Measure your distance from the goal, so you can plot your progress. Conduct polls to know where you stand with the public.

9. Carry out a diversionary attack, then attack elswhere. In a debate, ask your opponent several questions on one topic, then switch suddenly to another.

10. Prepare your development; don't aim directly at the goal. Set up a campaign organization, recruit volunteer workers, and otherwise prepare before you try to directly influence voters.

11. Make sure there is not immediate threat of your losing. Be sure that your nominating petition has many more signatures than you need, in case some are questioned.

15. Recognize patterns; know what to do with a pattern you recognize. Your candidate may be asked hundreds of different questions by reporters and by the voters. But underneath all these questions are a few basic patterns of concerns: national defense, crime, tax reduction, and the like. Prepare a response for each category. When you recognize the pattern, give the appropriate response.

22. If the game isn't working, change the rules. Instead of being against all the others, form a coalition with some of them.

These situations—deciding on college courses, trying for a job promotion, or running a political campaign—are all very different from each other. Yet in each one, you can apply strategic principles from games.

Of course, the applications don't come to you automatically. You must use your imagination to see which strategic principles apply as you meet each new situation. With practice, you can make this transfer more and more easily. Here are some questions you can ask yourself to get your imagination going:

1. Do you have an "opponent" in this situation?

2. Do you want to "destroy" your opponent or remain on good terms with your opponent afterwards?

3. Which strategies worked for other people in this situation?

4. Which strategies have worked for you in the past?

5. Is there something you can identify as a "move" in this situation?

6. Does the order of the "moves" matter?

7. What is a winning position?

8. What position leads to a winning position?

We have just given you some specific pointers about applying principles from deductive logic, inductive logic, and from strategy to life situations. You should realize, of course, that each game you've played, no matter what chapter it's in, draws on many different skills. For example, the 20 Questions game in deductive logic also requires strategic skills (planning your questions), and creative thinking (coming up with good questions).

Each life situation you face also draws on many different skills. The games in this book teach you these skills, as well as *systematic habits of thought* and *organized ways of approaching a task*. From strategy games, for example, you learn to plan how to reach your objectives, how to anticipate your opponent's moves, and how to benefit from your experiences. To appreciate this point better, let's look at still another situation and see how the various skills and systematic habits of thought you can learn from this book can be applied.

Suppose you are selling your car; the "opponent" is a potential buyer who has answered your ad.

1. *Plan how to reach your objectives.* Decide what the car's best selling points are, so you can be sure to emphasize them. For example, fuel prices might be high, and the car is very economical to run. Therefore (by using deduction), your car is a good one to buy. You will be sure to mention this to buyers.

2. *Anticipate your opponent's moves.* You must be prepared if the potential buyer says: "Will you guarantee that the car will pass state inspection? . . . You're asking $700; I'll give you $600. . . . Could I have my mechanic check out the car?"

3. *Learn from your experiences.* Suppose you realize that four people who have looked at your car have said, "I'll let you know,"—and have not returned.

Each has commented that the rust spots look bad. You realize (by using induction) that the rust spots are getting in the way of a sale, and you get the rust spots removed before you show the car to someone else.

## SPECIAL TIPS FOR PARENTS AND TEACHERS

You may be one of many parents whose child has trouble in a particular school subject, such as mathematics, or whose child is generally not interested in schoolwork. As a teacher, you are even more likely to have some students who fit these descriptions. As a parent or teacher, you will find many benefits from playing games with your child or students. You will not only understand them better, but you will also communicate with them better though playing games. Here are some special pointers:

1. As a parent, you might use the book to play games with your younger children, or you may introduce your children to the book if they are old enough to use it on their own. Encourage them to transfer what they learn from the games to their lives, to make plans, to eliminate possibilities, and so on. The purpose is for them to get the full benefit of improvement of their thinking skills. And do the same yourself!

2. As a teacher, you can use the book as a guide to teaching thinking. Introduce games at the level you think will be appropriate for your class, and be prepared to change this level as you see how the class progresses. Remember that it's easier to break one or two sticks than a whole bunch at once: Don't start with something too difficult. Be sure to follow up after playing games in a particular group by applying the principles to other school subjects, especially mathematics and language arts. You can suggest that, as homework, your students apply what they have learned from the games in their out-of-school lives, and report back to the class.

3. As a parent or teacher, you can use this book in a diagnostic way with your child or student. It gives a kind of information that IQ tests do not: It shows directly how well the child functions in some important

skill areas, and how quickly the child improves in these areas with practice. By observing the child's play, you also get information about the child's personality (for example, how well the child accepts defeat) and the child's communication skills. A game-playing environment is a safe one for dealing with the child's needs and modifying his or her behavior.

Try out games from each of the major chapters to see where the child is weakest. You then know which group of games to encourage the child to play more often. Keep track of the child's strongest area too. When the child needs an ego boost, you can play a game in that area.

Keep in mind that, as a parent or a teacher, it's no shame to be beaten in a game by a child. A child may think faster or remember better than an adult. A child may be more free from the stereotyped ways of thinking that blind an older person. When you are beaten, be proud that you are helping a child to develop his or her thinking ability.

# Appendices

—A warm-up exercise game
—How to apply permutations, combinations and
    probability to games
—Bridge

## A WARM-UP EXERCISE GAME

Before running a race, an athlete does stretching exercises to warm up. Before you play the games in this book, you may want to do a little mental warming-up (WU) with the following games.

---

## WU 1–1 (LL)
### RULES OF THE GAME

*Aim of the Game*: To reach as close as possible to a two-digit number by addition, subtraction, multiplication, and division of the numbers 1 through 6.

*Number of Players*: One or more

*Materials Needed*: Two decks of cards; pencil and paper.

*Preparation*: From the first deck, shuffle together a 2 through 6 to form pile A; shuffle together a 1 through 10 to form pile B. Draw one card from each pile to form the target number: the pile A card gives the value of the *tens* place, and the pile B card the value of the *units* place. A "10" drawn from pile B counts as a *zero*.

*How to Play*: From the second deck, each player is dealt an ace through six. The player must add, subtract, multiply, and/or divide the numbers on some or all of these cards to reach a result as close as possible to the target number. The player writes down his/her solution.

*Scoring*: Player who comes closest to the target number, either above or below it, gets one point. In case of a tie, the player who reaches a solution *first* gets the point.

## WU 1–2 (ML)

Same as WU 1–1, but pile A contains 5–9, instead of 2–6, so that target number will be between 50 and 99, instead of between 20 and 69. Each player is given six cards chosen at random from a pile of 1–10 to work with, instead of being given a pile of 1–6 to work with.

## WU 1–3 (HL)

Same as WU 1–1, but the player must make use of *all* six cards in the solution, instead of having the choice of using only *some* of the cards.

Let's look first at how a game of WU 1–1 might go: Suppose a 2 is drawn from pile A, and a 7 from pile B. Then the target number is 27. Players could reach 27 exactly in a lot of ways, for example:

$$(6 \times 5) - 3$$
$$(1 + 2 + 6) \times 3$$
$$(6 \times 4) + 3$$
$$[ (5 + 2) \times 4] - 1$$

Here's another sample game of WU 1–1. If a 5 is drawn from pile A and a 7 from pile B, then the target number is 57. Players could reach 57 exactly in a lot of ways, for example:

$$(6 \times 5 \times 2) - 3$$
$$(5 \times 4 \times 3) - 2 - 1$$
$$(6 + 2) (4 + 3) + 1$$

Now here's a sample game of WU 1–2. Suppose the target number is 76, and the six cards a player is given are 1, 2, 3, 5, 6, and 8. Here are some of the solutions the player might come up with:

$$(8 + 1) (6 + 2) + 3 \qquad = 75, \text{ one away}$$
$$(8 + 1) (6 + 2) + 5 \qquad = 77, \text{ one away}$$
$$[ (8 + 6 + 2) \times 5] - 3 - 1 = 76 \text{ exactly}$$

Finally, here's a sample game of WU 1–1, when the target number is 43. The player might use all six cards to reach it these ways:

$$6 \times (4 + 2) + 5 + 3 - 1$$
$$[(6 \times 5 \times 4) / (1 + 2)] + 3$$

## PROBABILITY, COMBINATIONS, AND PERMUTATIONS

Certain simple but powerful mathematical ideas underly some of the games in this book. Let's briefly introduce a few ideas of permutations, combinations, and probability as they apply to some of the games in the Deductive Logic chapter. A *permutation* is an ordering of objects. "123" is a different permutation than "132." A *combination* is a grouping of objects. "122" is the same combination as "212." *Probability* tells you the chances an event will occur. "There's a twenty percent chance of rain tomorrow." This introduction may help you to play better and also stimulate you to learn more mathematics and enjoy doing it.

Suppose we are playing game D 5–1, to find the rank and position of two out of five cards (with duplication allowed). How many different secret codes are there? One way to find out is to list them all. Here they are:

$$
\begin{array}{ccccc}
11 & 21 & 31 & 41 & 51 \\
12 & 22 & 32 & 42 & 52 \\
13 & 23 & 33 & 43 & 53 \\
14 & 24 & 34 & 44 & 54 \\
15 & 25 & 35 & 45 & 55
\end{array}
$$

There are 25 different secret codes, each of which is called a *permutation*.

Let's look more closely at the systematic way we have listed them.

The first column shows all five possibilities where a 1 is the first card. The next column shows all five possibilities where a 2 is the first card. Since there are five different possibilities for the first card, and since each leads to five different possibilities for the second card, we see that all together there are $5 \times 5 = 25$ different secret codes.

By using this systematic approach of listing the possibilities we can be confident that we don't miss any. We can also see a short-cut way to find out how many different secret codes there are: We multiply the number of different cards there can be in the first position by the number of different cards there can be in the second position: $5 \times 5 = 25$.

We can use this kind of short-cut with the other games of the same family (some out of many). For example, if the purpose of D 5–2 is to find the rank and position of three out of five cards, then there are $5 \times 5 \times 5 = 125$ different possible secret codes.

Do you see why? Suppose we list just those codes which have a 1 in the first position:

$$
\begin{array}{ccccc}
111 & 121 & 131 & 141 & 151 \\
112 & 122 & 132 & 142 & 152 \\
113 & 123 & 133 & 143 & 153 \\
114 & 124 & 134 & 144 & 154 \\
115 & 125 & 135 & 145 & 155
\end{array}
$$

There are 25 of them—the same 25 we listed for the two out of five game, but now we have put a 1 in front of each. And there are another 25 just like them but with a 2 in the first position, another 25 with a 3 in the first position, and so on. All together, then, there are 5 × 5 × 5 = 125 different secret codes.

Using the same short-cut, we can set up a table showing how many different secret codes are possible for other some-out-of-many games:

SOME OUT OF MANY
Number of Cards in Code

|  |  | 3 | 4 | 5 |
|---|---|---|---|---|
|  | 6 | 216 | 1296 | 7776 |
|  | 7 | 343 | 2401 | 16807 |
| Number of Possible | 8 | 512 | 4096 | 32768 |
| Cards | 9 | 729 | 6561 | 59049 |
|  | 10 | 1000 | 10000 | 100000 |

Let's focus now on the game D 5–3, four out of six. From what we have already learned, we can say there are 1296 different possible secret codes (6 × 6 × 6 × 6). We won't attempt to list them all. But let's see if we can put them into groups. Here's one way to group the 1296 different codes:

| Group 1 | Group 2 | Group 3 | Group 4 | Group 5 |
|---|---|---|---|---|
| 1234 | 1233 | 1112 | 1122 | 1111 |
| 1256 | 1125 | 2444 | 1144 | 2222 |
| 2345 | 3445 | 2333 | 2266 | 3333 |
| etc. | etc. | etc. | etc. | etc. |

Do you see the rule for what secret code goes in which group? (Here's a chance to apply your Inductive Logic skills.) In Group 1, each card in a code is different from every other card in the same code. In Group 2, each code contains a pair of the same cards, and two other cards different from the pair and from each other. In Group 3, each code contains a triplet (three same cards), and one card different from the triplet. Group 4 contains two different pairs in each code. Group 5 contains all the same cards in each code. Each of the 1296 different secret cards in the game D 5–3 fits into one of these groups.

An interesting question now is how many different codes belong to each group. Knowing the answer might help you to plan your strategy in playing this game. It's easy to see how many different codes fit into Group 5. There are just six: 1111, 2222, 3333, 4444, 5555, and 6666.

How about Group 1? Do you see a way to get the answer without listing them all and then counting? For each code in Group 1, the first position may contain any one of six cards. But since each card must be different from the others in the code, the second position may contain any one of only five. The third position must contain a card different from the first two, so there are only *four* possibilities. The fourth position must contain a card different from the first three, so there are only three possibilities. All together there are $6 \times 5 \times 4 \times 3 = 360$ different secret codes of the Group 1 type.

How about Group 2 now? Do you see a way to get the answer without listing them all and then counting? The pair in each code of Group 2 may be any one of six: 11, 22, 33, 44, 55, or 66. And it may occur in any one of six positions:

$$
\begin{array}{cccc}
X & X & \_ & \_ \\
X & \_ & X & \_ \\
X & \_ & \_ & X \\
\_ & X & X & \_ \\
\_ & X & \_ & X \\
\_ & \_ & X & X \\
\end{array}
$$

So six different pairs are possible, in any of six different positions, for a total of $6 \times 6 = 36$ possibilities. But then we have two more cards to consider in each code; they must be different from the pair and different from each other. The first can be any one of five cards (any one but the pair card), and, once it is chosen, the second can be any one of four cards. So all together we have $6 \times 6 \times 5 \times 4 = 720$ different codes of the Group 2 type.

How about Group 3? The triplet can be any one of six (111, 222, 333, 444, 555, or 666). The other card can be any one of five, and it can be in any one of four positions. So we have $6 \times 5 \times 4 = 120$ different codes of the Group 3 type.

Can you see how to figure out the number of possibilities for Group 4? The first pair can be any one of six (11, 22, 33, 44, 55, or 66). Once it is chosen the second pair can be any one of five. The arrangement of the two pairs can be any one of three:

| | |
|---|---|
| Side by side | A  A  B  B |
| Alternating | A  B  A  B |
| or "books and bookends" | A  B  B  A |

So we have 6 × 5 × 3 = 90 different codes of the Group 4 type.

Here's a summary of our results:

| Group | Example | Number of Secret Codes | Probability |
|---|---|---|---|
| 1 | 1 2 3 4 | 360 | .28 |
| 2 | 1 2 3 3 | 720 | .56 |
| 3 | 1 2 2 2 | 120 | .09 |
| 4 | 1 1 2 2 | 90 | .07 |
| 5 | 1 1 1 1 | 6 | — |

To find the *probability* that a code chosen at random falls into a particular group, you divide the number of secret codes for that group by 1296, the total number of secret codes. We have done this and listed the results into the last column of our table. You may be suprised to learn that there are twice as many codes in Group 2 as in Group 1. When the code is chosen by chance, therefore, it is twice as likely to be of Group 2 than of Group 1.

Let's look next at the family of games where you must find the rank *but not position* of some out of many. For example, in game D 2–1, you must find the ranks of two out of five. How many secret codes are there? We already know that, for game D 5–1, where you have to find both the rank and position, there are 5 × 5 = 25 different secret codes. For 5 of these 25 codes, both cards are the same: 11, 22, 33, 44, and 55.

Let's think now about those other 20 codes where both cards are different. For each of these codes, there is another just like it but with the order reversed: for 12, there is also 21; for 35, there is also 53; and so on. In other words, only half of these 20 secret codes, or 10, are *different* when only rank is important. So all together there are 15 (5 + 10) different secret codes when you must find the rule but not the position of two out of five.

Each different secret code is called a *combination*. For two out of five, with *rank and position*, there are 25 *permutations*; but with two out of five, *rank only*, there are 15 combinations.

You've just been given a very short introduction to:

1. *Permutations*: How many different secret codes of rank and position are possible with two out of five?
2. *Probability*: What are the chances in four out of six that the secret code is in Group 1?
3. *Combinations*: How many different secret codes of rank alone are possible with 2 out of 5?

You can both have fun and make use of these mathematical topics when you explore them in connection with the games of this book.

## WHIST

Each player has been the opponent of every other player in the games of this book. Before introducing the widely played game of Bridge, which pits a team of two players against another team of two partners, let's start with the simpler game of Whist.

---

### SC 27-1 (LL)
**RULES OF THE GAME**

*Aim of the Game*: To win more "tricks" than the other team when trumps are determined at random.

*Number of Players*: Four; two teams of two each.

*Materials Needed*: Deck of cards.

*Preparation*: Each player draws a card from the shuffled deck. Those with the two highest cards become partners and sit opposite each other, with one player from the other team on either side. The player drawing the highest card is the dealer.

The complete deck is shuffled, and the dealer deals out all the cards face down, one at a time, in a clockwise order beginning with the player on the dealer's left, until the last card, called the *trump* card, which is dealt face up. All cards of the same suit as that of the trump card are called "trumps." Except for the trump card, players hold their cards in their hands so that only they can see their cards. Just before the dealer's first turn to play, he or she picks up the trump card as part of his or her hand.

*How to Play*: Each player in clockwise order plays one card face up in the center of the table. The player on the dealer's left "leads" by playing *any* card; all the other players must in turn play a card of the same suit if they have one; if not, they can play *any* card.

The four cards played are called a *trick*. If no trumps have been played in the trick, the highest card of the suit led wins the trick. If one or more trumps have been played in the trick, the player who played the highest trump wins the trick. The winner of a trick leads on the next trick.

One player from each team keeps to the side all the tricks won by that team. No player may look again at those cards during the game.

The game continues until all the cards have been played (13 tricks).

*Scoring*: A team gets one point for each trick won above six.

---

Here's how a game might begin: Suppose the players are called South, West, North, and East, according to their positions around the table, with South and North one team and East and West the other. South deals the following cards to each player, with the 5D being the trump card. You as the reader can see everybody's cards, but each player can see only his or her own cards and, at the beginning, the trump card.

1. On the first trick, West leads the 4S, North plays the 9S, East the KS, and South the 3S. Since no trumps were played, East wins the trick with the king.

2. As winner of the last trick, East leads the 4C. South plays the JC, West the KC, and North the AC.

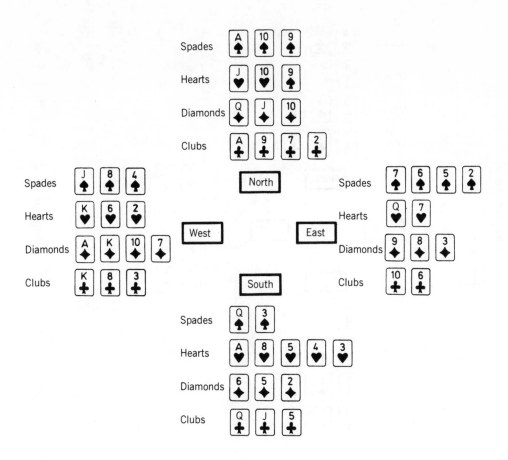

Spades: A 10 9
Hearts: J 10 9
Diamonds: Q J 10
Clubs: A 9 7 2

North

Spades: J 8 4
Hearts: K 6 2
Diamonds: A K 10 7
Clubs: K 8 3

West

Spades: 7 6 5 2
Hearts: Q 7
Diamonds: 9 8 3
Clubs: 10 6

East

South

Spades: Q 3
Hearts: A 8 5 4 3
Diamonds: 6 5 2
Clubs: Q J 5

3. As winner of the last trick, North now leads the 9H, East plays the QH, South the AH, and West the 2H.

4. South leads the 3H, West plays the 6H, North the JH, and East the 7H.

5. Since the North–South team has been successful with two heart tricks, North now leads another heart, the 10H. East has no hearts, and chooses to play the 3D, one of the *trump* cards. If no one else plays a trump card on this trick, East will win. South plays the 4H, and West the KH. East has played the only trump on this trick and wins. But it turns out that East's trump was wasted, because his partner West's KH would have won the trick if East had chosen to play a club or spade.

237

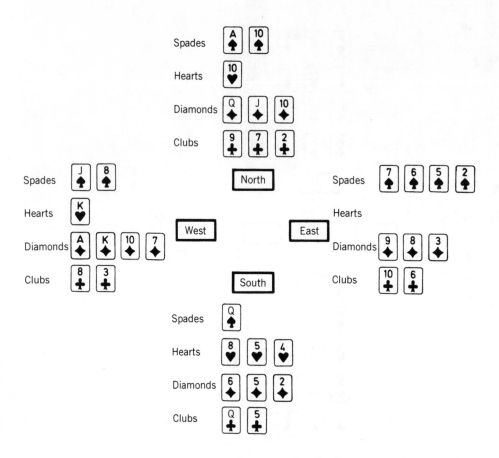

Spades: A♠ 10♠
Hearts: 10♥
Diamonds: Q♦ J♦ 10♦
Clubs: 9♣ 7♣ 2♣

North

West

East

South

Spades (West): J♠ 8♠
Hearts (West): K♥
Diamonds (West): A♦ K♦ 10♦ 7♦
Clubs (West): 8♣ 3♣

Spades (East): 7♠ 6♠ 5♠ 2♠
Hearts (East):
Diamonds (East): 9♦ 8♦ 3♦
Clubs (East): 10♣ 6♣

Spades (South): Q♠
Hearts (South): 8♥ 5♥ 4♥
Diamonds (South): 6♦ 5♦ 2♦
Clubs (South): Q♣ 5♣

6. East now leads the 6C. South plays the QC, West the 3C, and North the 2C.

7. South, the winner of the last trick, has counted that eleven hearts have already been played and knows that no other player has any hearts left. South leads the 5H, hoping that partner North will have a high trump to win with.

West has the *highest* trumps, the ace and the king, but realizes that these will *always* be winning cards when they are played, so chooses to play the 8C. North plays the JD (trumps). East has no hearts, the suit led, and only *lower* trumps than the jack. So East plays the 10C.

The situation now looks like this:

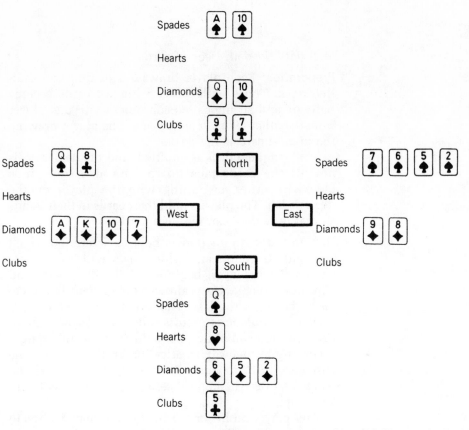

Spades A♠ 10♠

Hearts

Diamonds Q♦ 10♦

Clubs 9♣ 7♣

North

Spades Q♠ 8♣

Hearts

Diamonds A♦ K♦ 10♦ 7♦

Clubs

West — East

Spades 7♠ 6♠ 5♠ 2♠

Hearts

Diamonds 9♦ 8♦

Clubs

South

Spades Q♠

Hearts 8♥

Diamonds 6♦ 5♦ 2♦

Clubs 5♣

The game continues as follows, with the winning card in each trick underlined:

|    | West | North | East | South |
|----|------|-------|------|-------|
| 8. | 8S | 10S (led) | 2S | _QS_ |
| 9. | JS | _QD_ | 5S | 8H (led) |
| 10. | _7D_ | AS (led) | 6S | 5C |
| 11. | _AD_ (led) | 4D | 8D | 2D |
| 12. | _KD_ (led) | 7C | 9D | 5D |
| 13. | 10D (led) | 9C | 7S | 6D |

North–South have won seven tricks all together. They receive 7 − 6 = 1 point.

**SIMPLE BRIDGE**

## SC 28–1 (ML)

**RULES OF THE GAME**

*Aim of the Game*: To win more "tricks" than the other team when trumps are determined by bidding.

*Number of Players*: Four, two teams of two each.

*Materials Needed*: Deck of cards.

*Preparation*: Each player draws a card from the shuffled deck. Those with the two highest cards become partners and sit opposite each other, with one player from the other team on either side. The player drawing the highest card is the dealer.

The complete deck is shuffled, and the dealer deals out all the cards face down, one at a time, in a clockwise order, beginning with the player on the dealer's left. The players hold their cards in their hands so that only they can see their cards.

*How to Play*: An *auction* is held to determine which suit will be trumps and which team will become *declarers*. Each player, beginning with the dealer and continuing clockwise, is allowed to bid. Each bid has to be higher than the last. The *lowest* bid is *clubs*, followed by *diamonds*, *hearts*, *spades*, and *no trump*. (You can remember that the suits increase in strength according to their alphabetical order: C, D, H, S). The strongest bid, "no trump," means that no suit will be trump and that the highest card of the suit led will win each trick.

Any player on his or her turn to bid may decline to make a bid by saying "pass" instead of naming a suit or no trump.

The bidding continues until:

1. one player bids "no trump," or
2. three players pass in a row (everyone agrees to the last bid).

If, however, the *first* four bids are all "pass," the hand is cancelled, and the cards are shuffled and re-dealt by the player on the dealer's left.

The team that makes the last bid of a suit or of no trump are called "declarers" and the other team "defenders."

In clockwise order, each player plays one card face up in the center of the table. The player to the left of the player who bid the trump suit (or no trump) "leads" by playing *any* card; all the other players must in turn play a card of the same suit if they have one; if not, they can play *any* card.

The four cards played are called a *trick*. If no trumps

have been played in the trick, the highest card of the suit led wins the trick. If one or more trumps have been played in the trick, the player who played the highest trump wins the trick. The winner of a trick leads on the next trick.

*Scoring*: The points awarded depend on whether *declarers* or *defenders* took more than six of the tricks and on what was trumps, as shown:

| Trumps | Declarers Took More Than Six Tricks | Defenders Took More Than Six Tricks |
|---|---|---|
| Clubs | 1 | 2 |
| Diamonds | 2 | 4 |
| Hearts | 3 | 6 |
| Spades | 4 | 8 |
| No Trump | 5 | 10 |

Suppose these are the cards dealt out:

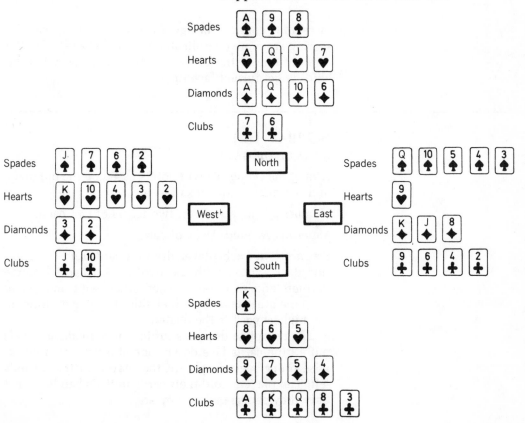

## CONTRACT BRIDGE

South, as dealer, has five clubs (including the A, K, and Q) and so bids clubs, hoping that the suit will become trumps. West bids hearts, since that is West's longest and strongest suit. North, holding four hearts (including the A, Q, and J), is happy to have hearts as trumps, and says "pass." East has some strength in each suit except hearts: East has four clubs, three diamonds (including the K and J), and five spades. East figures that partner West must have strength in hearts and that, together, the partnership will be best served by bidding "no trump." East does, and the bidding ends.

If the declarers (East and West) take more than six tricks, they will get five points. If the defenders (North and South) take more than six tricks, they will get ten points.

In regular contract bridge, both the bidding and the scoring are more complicated than in SC 22–1, and the cards of one of the players in the team that wins the bidding get turned face up.

## SC 29–1 (HL)
### RULES OF THE GAME

*Aim of the Game*: To win points based on the bid made and the number of tricks taken.

*Number of Players*: Four; two teams of two each.

*Materials Needed*: Deck of cards.

*Preparation*: Each player draws a card from the shuffled deck. Those with the two highest cards become partners and sit opposite each other, with one player from the other team on either side. The player drawing the highest card is the dealer.

The complete deck is shuffled, and the dealer deals out all the cards face down, one at a time, in a clockwise order beginning with the player on the dealer's left. The players hold their cards in their hands so that only they can see what they are.

*How to Play*: An *auction* is held to determine the trumps suit, the team to receive the *contract* and the size of the contract. A contract of one means that a team will try for one trick more than six; a contract of two means a team will try for two tricks more than six; and so on.

Each player, beginning with the dealer and continuing clockwise, is allowed to bid on what the trump suit should be. Each bid has to be higher than the last. The *lowest* bid is 1 *club,* followed by 1 *diamond,* 1 *heart,* 1 spade, 1 *no trump,* 2 *clubs,* 2 *diamonds,* 2 *hearts,* and so on. You can remember that the suits increase in strength according their alphabetical order: C, D, H, S. The strongest bid, "no trump," means that no suit will be trump, and that the highest card of the suit led will win each trick. A bid of one of something means that the team expects to take one more than six tricks, or seven all together; a bid of two means that the team expects to take two more than six tricks, or eight all together; and so it goes.

Any player on his or her turn to bid may decline to make a bid by saying "pass" instead of naming a suit or no trump.

A player may bid *double* following the last bid made by an opponent. This has the effect, if the doubled bid becomes the contract, of increasing the declarer's point score if the contract is fulfilled, but increasing the defender's point score if it isn't.

A player may bid *redouble* if the opposing team has doubled the bid of his or her team. This further increases the point score that the winning side (declarer, if they fulfill contract; defenders if they don't) will get.

The bidding ends when a bid, a double, or a redouble is followed by three passes in a row. The final bid becomes the contract, and the player who first bid the suit (or no trump) named in the contract becomes the *declarer*. The declarer's partner is called the *dummy*. The player on the other team are called *defenders*.

If, however, the *first* four bids are all "pass," the hand is cancelled, and the cards are shuffled and redealt by the player on the dealer's left.

Each player in clockwise order plays one card face up in the center of the table. The player on the declarer's left "leads" by playing *any* card; all the other players must in turn play a card of the same suit if they have one; if not, they can play *any* card.

After the first card is led, the *dummy's* cards are placed face up on the table. On each trick, the declarer chooses which card will be played from the dummy hand.

The four cards played are called a *trick*. If no trumps have been played in the trick, the highest card of the suit led wins the trick. If one or more trumps have been played in the trick, the player who played the highest trump wins the trick. The winner of a trick leads on the next trick.

*Scoring:* The points awarded depend in a complicated way on the final contract, on the number of tricks taken, and on the results of previous games. Many books on bridge can give you complete scoring tables, and examples of how the scoring tables apply to different situations. These books can also help you with strategies for bidding and playing the cards.